Our Partnership With China

EIR Contents

www.larouchepub.com Volume 44, Number 40, October 6, 2017

White House/Shealah Craighead

Cover This Week

President Donald Trump and President Xi Jinping at the G20 Summit in Hamburg, Germany, July 9, 2017.

OUR PARTNERSHIP WITH CHINA

I. The Land-Bridge in History

3 The Attack on Christopher Columbus: Irregular Warfare Against the New Silk Road
by Dennis Speed

8 Why Go to China?
by Michael G. Steger

12 The Choice Before Germany and Europe
by Helga Zepp-LaRouche

28 Columbus' First 'Belt and Road' Inspired by Cusa
by Will Wertz

32 Einstein Was Right: Only a Fool Keeps Repeating His Mistakes
by Helga Zepp-LaRouche

II. And in America Today

35 INTERVIEW Helga Zepp-LaRouche
China's Vision for a New Silk Road: A Nightmare for Evil People, But a Dream for Mankind

45 LAROUCHE PAC MANHATTAN MEETING
Americans Must Understand What China Is Really Doing

III. Actual Economics

51 Return to the Machine-Tool Principle
by Lyndon H. LaRouche, Jr.
January 22, 1997

66 Rebuild Puerto Rico and All North America with 'New Silk Road' Paradigm
by Marcia Merry Baker and Paul Gallagher

The Attack on Christopher Columbus: Irregular Warfare Against the New Silk Road

by Dennis Speed

Oct. 1—The intelligence warfare being waged by British imperial forces against the integration of the United States, China and Russia into a single "World Land-Bridge" as a new economic platform is currently being flanked by Lyndon LaRouche and his co-thinkers "on the culture front." Now that the attack on the Presidency by the FBI has been accurately placed in its proper context by the La-Rouche dossier on Robert Mueller, a new front is being opened up in the war to bring the United States into the World Land-Bridge as a partner with those two "continental" nations, thus thwarting the danger of thermonuclear war. Following the release last week of the "Open Letter to President Donald Trump in Defense of Columbus" by Liliana Gorini, leader of the *Movisol* organization in Italy, American artists, political figures, historians, and citizens have begun an animated re-investigation of the origins and purpose of the voyages of Christopher Columbus. Through new and newly reconsidered historical documents, the Columbian expeditions are being re-situated in the context of the alliance that is now possible among Presidents Trump, Putin and Xi Jinping.

Addressing a New York City meeting on September 30, Helga Zepp-LaRouche, founder of the Schiller Institute, and known for more than twenty years as "the Silk Road Lady" because of her tireless campaigning for the economic policy now known as the World Land-Bridge, said:

Flor de la Mar, *a 16th century Portuguese carrack, like Columbus' largest ship, the* Santa Maria.

Some of you may remember that a couple of months ago, at a meeting in New York at which the Chinese Ambassador in Washington, Cui Tiankai, gave a presentation, he said that there were sixteen examples in history in which a country surpassed the then dominant power: that in twelve cases it led to war, and in four cases, the rising power just replaced the old dominant power.

Ambassador Cui said that China wants neither a future like one of the twelve cases in which war ensued, nor a future like that of the other four cases, because what China is offering is a completely new model of relations among states.

I want to go through this because I think it is absolutely key. China is proposing a new model for major powers, based on absolute respect for the sovereignty of the other states—including the principle of non-interference, the principle of the acceptance of another social model, and a win-win cooperation between the two of them.

A new diplomacy, free of geopolitics, based on a shared community of scientific principle: This is the future for the world if so desired by the United States. Celebrating the best of each culture's contributions to world civilization, and a dialogue among all cultures, is a most effective way to initiate that diplomacy, and this has been the mission of the Schiller Institute since its inception. Fundamentally, that was also the mission of the Columbus voyages, as conceived by their originator, Nicholas of Cusa, friend of the Toscanelli who provided the maps to Christopher Columbus. It is this outlook which is the true target of the attack on Columbus. And just as British intelligence deployed Jacobin mobs to destroy France, so today Antifa and other forces are deployed to destroy the capability for this new dialogue of civilizations.

The New Khmer Rouge

The past decades have seen an intensification in the worldwide destruction of irreplaceable cultural artifacts as ostensibly "collateral damage" in warfare: the Baghdad Museum, the artifacts of Palmyra, the books of Timbuktu. In this destruction, the active hand of British intelligence, as well as the Malthusian cultural outlook of British-affiliated oligarchical forces is manifest. Such was the moral disposition that expressed itself in the firebombing of Dresden and the destruction of other targets of little military value during the Second World War. "Antifa," Boko Haram, ISIS and other organizations are the fronts for this organized assault on the cultural memory and heritage of humanity as a whole.

A 225 year-old monument to Christopher Columbus, the oldest in the United States, was smashed in Baltimore, Maryland on August 21. On Aug. 30, in Yonkers, New York, a statue of Columbus was beheaded. On Sept. 12 a Columbus statue was defaced in Central Park. In Columbus Circle, New York City, on September 23, the hands of Columbus were painted. Just as in 1793 France, when the terrorist fanatics that beheaded statues of prophets and saints at the Cathedral of Notre Dame referred to themselves as "The Cult of Reason," so today's fascist "Antifa" has declared that

Statue of Christopher Columbus by Gaetano Russo, Columbus Circle, New York City.

Oct. 9 will be "Deface Columbus Day," using slogans like "the future is racial and economic justice."

While they claim to be defending others "against racial and economic injustice," Antifa's roots are with the Ku Klux Klan and the anti-Italian campaigns in the America of 125 years ago. In an Aug. 25 op-ed in *The Hill* newspaper, authors J. P. McCusker and Patrick Korten of the National Christopher Columbus Association wrote:

In the 1920s, from coast to coast, members of the Ku Klux Klan opposed Columbus. In Richmond, they tried to stop the erection of a Columbus monument. In Pennsylvania, they burned fiery crosses to threaten those celebrating Columbus. The Klan newspaper, *The American Standard*, attacked honoring Columbus—on the basis that a holiday for him was some sort of papal plot. The Klan was no fan of Columbus.

There is no reason to assume that the dupes, in or supporting Antifa, know any of this, since there is no reason to assume that they know anything. There is also no reason to assume that since George Soros simultaneously supports right wing Ukrainian fascists (who indeed do use the Confederate flag as a symbol of white supremacy) and Black Lives Matter—to the order of tens of millions of dollars—that the Soros funding conduit is not flowing in all directions in this case as well. Reversing the ongoing assault on human civilization in the form of the defacing and beheading of Columbus statues is best undertaken by using this present circumstance to probe Friedrich Schiller's question: "What Is, and To What End Do We Study, Universal History?"

Columbus, Cusa, and the World Land-Bridge

In the past two weeks, a re-investigation by Will Wertz and others, of extant materials regarding the fifteenth century cultural interchange between the "city-builders," astronomers, artisans and machinists of Florence, and the scholars, ship-builders and navigators of China, has established something that is simultaneously of exciting historical significance, as well as urgent importance to the immediate future of the United States. It is, that the 1492 Columbian mission to China, involving advanced knowledge of techniques for the circumnavigation of the globe, and entrusted to Columbus in the 1470's, was discussed by Paolo Toscanelli with Chinese scholars as early as 1433. The Columbus mission was never merely to discover a "westward path to the east," for purposes of trade. Rather, it was intended to create the basis to re-establish, if necessary, a failing European civilization in another location on the planet, free of the corruption of the "Old World," and to initiate a dialogue on the most advanced principles of machine design, navigation and invention itself with a civilization potentially as, or more, advanced than that of Europe. The extraordinary Ming Dynasty fleet, which ruled the world's known waterways for a quarter century (1405-1433) and dwarfed anything that would be seen from Europe for the next 400 years, demonstrated the scientific capabilities of that civilization.

It must, however, also be noted that in the Florence of those years, there was a qualitative difference, a new, unique accomplishment, one that would have already greeted the Chinese scholars that traveled to the Florence in 1433. A fundamental revolution in science had been effected by Cardinal Nicholas of Cusa, Filippo Brunelleschi, Paolo Toscanelli and others, which did not exist anywhere else in the world. This was their, and specifically Cusa's, investigation of the creative principle of discovery itself. This was expressed in the three-fold process of Nicholas of Cusa's book *On Learned Ignorance*, the building of the Brunelleschi dome, and the Cusa-proposed mission to the New World, an extension of his work to unify the world through the Council of Florence.

Toscanelli lived from 1397 until 1482, and was

Ships of Zheng He's fleet in an artist's rendition.

closely associated with Brunelleschi, Cusa, Leonardo da Vinci, Columbus, and others. The "machine-tool principle" was expressed in the various machines invented by Brunelleschi (recorded in drawings by his friend Mariano Taccola, 1382-1453), and was expressed in Toscanelli's own astronomical inventions and experimental observations. Cusa's *De Docta Ignorantia* was written by 1439 and transformed all of the science and theology before his time. That, in turn, informed and advanced the knowledge of his perpetual interlocutors, who together shared, once Cusa formulated it, his mission: "Ever to the West."

It is the implications of this, the true mission of Columbus, for the United States of 2017, and for the future of the United States that embraces the World Land-Bridge idea, that the "anti-Columbus" campaign is intended to attack. For example, Lyndon LaRouche's design of his Four Laws, including the "Fourth Law" emphasis on new Physical principles, on thermonuclear fusion for space flight, and on industrializing the Moon, including mining it for Helium-3, are the proper basis for a new diplomacy involving China, Russia, India, Japan, South Africa and all nations in a new world arrangement, never before seen or created. If Americans understand that it is this, the very historic mission that brought this nation into existence, that is under assault in the attacks on Columbus, they will also understand how to use the vigorous defense of Columbus to move the World Land-Bridge policy into place as America's future. "Ever, Ever to th' West!"

Dvorak and Columbus

by Dennis Speed

Oct. 1—Twenty-five years ago, in 1992, a collection of essays entitled *Dvorak in America 1892-1895* was released (John C Tibbetts, ed., Timber Press, 1993) to commemorate the 100th anniversary of Dvorak's coming to America, and American Jeannette Thurber's attempt to create a National Conservatory of Music in the United States. Thurber, a thorough-going supporter of the idea of Classical composition as the birthright of all Americans, sought to deploy Dvorak as the champion of a new American "great and noble school of music." Notably, she saw Dvorak's mission to America as being identical in spirit and purpose with the Columbian mission. To that end, Dvorak brought the Classical tradition, only represented in Europe at that time by Giuseppe Verdi, Johannes Brahms, and himself, to the shores of America. The enforcement of a racist policy at the Metropolitan Opera prevented Dvorak from performing there, since both he and Thurber insisted on instruction in, and performance of Classical music by students of African-American and Indian descent, as well as women. The classical principles of composition were not only *for* all people—Classical music could and should be composed and performed *by* all people.

Dvorak composed several works for America, the most famous of which became his symphony number nine, "From the New World." Thurber, intent on forcing the Congress of the United States and the entire nation to support her concept of an American National Conservatory of classical music, also devised a specific "Columbus theme" for Dvorak. The following is excerpted from the essay, "The choral works: *Te Deum* and *The American Flag*," by Nick Strimple:

Statue of Antonin Dvorak in Stuyvesant Square Park, New York City.

When Antonin Dvorak arrived in New York on 27 September, 1892 to assume his duties as director of the National Conservatory, he had with him a new *Te Deum* and the piano sketch of a cantata, "The American Flag." Both works were brain children of the Conservatory's benefactor, Jeannette Thurber. Mrs. Thurber had thought that her new director should provide some suitable new work for the Columbus Quadricentennial Celebration scheduled for 12 October. It was at that concert that Dvorak would be officially "introduced" to the New World. Even though she had hatched this idea in the autumn of 1891, she had not provided any concrete suggestions until June 1892. At that time, Dvorak was requested to set to music one of the great ecclesiastical texts of jubilation, since an appropriate patriotic text had not been found … Within a month he received a copy of Joseph Rodman Drake's poem, "The American Flag." On 28 July he again wrote Mrs. Thurber:

"In my last letter I informed you that I would write a *Te Deum* and now I am able to say that it is completed and in a few days I will send it to you.

"If you wish to have it performed on the occasion of my first appearance in New York, on October 12, together with my *Triple Overture* it would be necessary to get it copied immediately. As to *The American Flag* by Joseph Rodman Drake (and the explanatory notes by his grandson Charles de Kay), I can tell you that I like the poem very much—it is really a grand poem—and your selection for a patriotic hymn—*Columbus Cantata*—is very well fitted for music.

"But what a pity it is that you did not send me the words a month earlier. It is quite impossible to get ready a work which will take half an hour in time for performance for October, and so I was compelled to write a *Te Deum*. I shall, however, go on with the work from which every musician must get inspired. Meantime, with many kind regards, I am faithfully yours,

Antonin Dvorak"

Dvorak began work on The American Flag almost immediately; he completed the piano sketch before he left Europe on Sept. 17.

Col. Thomas Wentworth Higginson, the first leader of an African-American regiment after Lincoln's 1863 Emancipation Proclamation, gave a speech in Dvorak's honor at Carnegie Hall, reported in the *New York Herald*, Oct. 22, 1892:

Jeannette Thurber

Over all this wide land to-day men and women have been celebrating the finding of this continent with such zeal you would think that each one had a hand in the discovery… It is fitting that music should take her part in the great festival because music is the only art which, since Columbus, has also discovered a new world. We meet to celebrate that newer discovery, to lay upon the bier of Columbus the only wreath that has wholly blossomed since his time: the one art that is post-Columbian…

The triumphs of our own land in music, like most of our artistic triumphs, lie in the future, if anywhere. If we were all made of unmixed English blood, we might have long to wait for them. Moreover the material successes must come first. If you choose the picked young men of each college class and send them out on railroads art must wait, or if a man of commanding genius give half his energies to the building of steam engines and only the other half to making symphonies, the chances are that the steam engines may go at high pressure, but the symphonies will not. But we shall not always be thus one sided, and, moreover, we are not all of English blood.

… And we draw to-night on that wondrous country where, it used to be said, every child was tested early in the cradle to see whether he would choose the violin bow or the rifle with his baby hand, the country which has so identified itself with the fire of genius that Boyle O'Reilly makes the burden of his best lyric run thus:—

"I had rather live in Bohemia
Than in any other land."

Let us hope that our guest to-night will at least not share this opinion, that he may consent to transplantation and help add the new world of music to the continent which Columbus found.

cc/Ericd

Monument to Christopher Columbus in Genoa, Italy.

Why Go to China?

by Michael G. Steger

Oct. 3—Upon returning from his first trip to China, Sept. 17-21, for the People's Daily *Media Forum on the Belt and Road, Michael Steger offers these reflections on the state of the U.S. mission for scientific and industrial progress, relative to that of China.*

If you, the reader, ever get the chance, you should go to China. See for yourself the level of development. See for yourself the changes that have occurred within just twenty-five years, within the scope of this massive nation. With a dramatic geography changing quickly from arid coasts to jagged mountains, then barren desert, then rivers that flood annually across huge basins, then again stark mountains, and then to farmland, and again back to desert: These people have built a civilization over 5,000 years!

It is clear to all that China is now looking to play a role in the modern world. They are adept with new technology, and most Chinese are living right next door to typical western luxuries. Yet, their progress over these last forty, and especially these last twenty-five years, has achieved what can only be described as an intangible sense of mission: A sense of mission for progress that is now a shared value within the very fabric of their society, a mission that has been replaced in the western elites, over that same forty years, with a ubiquitous and casual cynicism characteristic of a drunken Faust.

EIRNS/Michael Steger

Michael Steger at the new concert hall in Dunhuang, China.

One cannot help but think of what Napoleon had said, "Let her sleep, for when she wakes, she will shake the world!" China has awakened, and she is certainly shaking the world. Perhaps most ironically, she is shaking the world with the best of western civilization. Yes, it is often draped in Asian ceremony and traditional customs, which are sometimes refreshing compared to our casual practicality. What stands out most, however, is China's sense of mission for real scientific and social

EIRNS/Michael Steger

Camel caravan at the oasis near Dunhuang.

progress, an energetic by-the-seat-of-your-pants playfulness, and a pride in their civilization, nation, and culture which touches their very hearts with happiness.

These characteristics remind one of the essence of Beethoven's pulsing sense of mission, or Benjamin Franklin's incessant and unrestrained playfulness, and even, on deeper reflection, of Plato's idealistic meritocratic Republic.

By no means has China reached the pinnacle of these expressions, but these poignant references, of the heights of European civilization, resonate far more strongly in China today, than in the West, where such ideas are attacked as racist, drab, or antiquated. Per-

EIRNS/Michael Steger

The tallest building in Beijing, under construction.

haps, today, China is the mirror to which the West can turn to rediscover its own beauty, its own soul for discovery, development, and exploration.

With the initiative of the Belt and Road, China has called upon the world, and perhaps, even more specifically, upon the United States, to join in cooperation with the great civilization of the East for a project of Global Development, enriching all of mankind with the greatest mankind has to offer.

We must say yes to this collaboration. For ourselves, and for the entire world, it is today not an option, but an immediate necessity.

People's Daily Media Forum on the Belt and Road

Flying west from Beijing to Dunhuang, a three-hour flight across most of northern China, the landscape is more similar to the western United States than it is to the rich farmlands of our Midwest or the origins of industry in the hills and rivers of our Northeast.

The *People's Daily* is the largest circulation newspaper in China, and has been coordinating its coverage with Government policies since its first publication in 1948. It has a daily print circulation of 30 million. Its new online platform, including social media, which has been developed to a state-of-the-art facility over the last two years, now reaches 300 to 600 million people each day. It intends to expand this platform for a growing international audience.

In September and November 2013, President Xi announced the New Silk Road policy of China, first in Kazakhstan in September, and then in Indonesia in November 2013. Since then, China has shaped what is now known as the Belt and Road Initiative (BRI), including both over-ground rail and development corridors from east Asia to western Europe, as well as two maritime routes, through the Indian Ocean basin and the Mediterranean Sea, and another through the Arctic Ocean to northern Europe. By the end of this decade, the project will be twenty times the size of the Marshall Plan, the project which rebuilt Europe after World War II—or, in other words, the BRI has quickly become the new gold standard for global development projects.

The U.N. has endorsed this audacious project now in its fourth year, as have the 66 nations which attended the inaugural BRI Beijing forum in May 2017, hosted personally by President Xi. Each year since President Xi's announcement, *People's Daily* has held a Media Forum on the BRI, inviting directors and editors-in-chief of major news agencies from around the world, in hope of expanding global coverage of this ambitious and globally important project.

As many readers of this weekly publication well know, *EIR*, the Schiller Institute, and the LaRouche organization internationally have been initiating, developing, and covering this project since our first publication of this program in *EIR* in 1992. But most of the other periodicals and daily newspapers of Europe and

Sand dunes at the oasis near Dunhuang.

the United States have not covered the project at all, in any honest or supportive way, ever.

With this year's *People's Daily* conference, the leadership of China hopes to change that!

Travelling the 2,000-Year-Old Silk Road

For its first three years, the conference was held in Beijing as a two-day conference.

This year, following growing international support, *People's Daily* held the conference in the far western reaches of the northwestern province of Gansu, with nearly 400 representatives from more than 120 nations. Gansu is located where the Gobi desert and the Takla makan desert meet, literally at the fork-in-the-road of the millennia-old Silk Road, that very road traveled by camel caravans bringing silk, porcelain, gunpowder, movable-type printing, and spices from the East, and algebra, metals, gems, and Mediterranean culture from the West.

The city of Dunhaung is located at a mirage-like oasis in the sand-covered desert, with a landscape unlike anything in the world. The sand dune mountains rise above the town of Dunhuang, surrounding an ancient freshwater oasis which is fed by underground reservoirs from ancient mountain runoff, and the Mogao caves, built between 400 and 900 A.D., are filled with ancient Buddhist temples sculpted from the ancient river's porous sandstone, then plastered and painted with the colors of Himalayan stone such as lapis lazuli, green copper, and onyx, as brilliant in color today as they were 1,000 years ago.

These legacies of the ancient Silk Road capture the vibrant culture, trade, and spirit that embodied the international richness of the ancient Silk Road. Today there are camel trains heading deep into the mountainous dunes as in millennia gone by, now letting tourists relive the ancient Silk Road—tourists who seek to experience this remarkable place.

Such was the start of the conference, with a day of reimagining.

The Message Is Clear

"China has taken the international responsibility to develop nations around the world. It is time for you to cover this project."

It is hard to say if the many western journalists un-

A camel caravan at the Dunhuang oasis.

derstand the scope or importance of this project, rather than it being simply something China is "doing." Many western journalists unfortunately have little understanding of physical economics, science and industry, agriculture, or infrastructure development. In short, most are simply not prepared to understand this project, and this goes as well for many others around the world today.

One might say that the current understanding of the BRI is similar to the understanding by the average American, or leading journalist, of John Kennedy's mission to land a man on the Moon. For most, that mission was simply a competitive feat to beat the Soviets. For the more enlightened, it was, and still remains, the only path to enduring peace through scientific development!

As is the BRI today.

However, after an intense day contemplating the ancient Silk Road, including a beautiful evening concert, followed the next day by a media forum with presentations by leading figures from many of China's thirty-two provinces—as well as presentations and panel discussions by leading figures of western, African, and Asian media agencies—some of this incomprehension began to change. Then, on returning to Beijing, all 400 participants convened in a summit in the Great Hall of the People with Vice Premier Zhang Gaoli, the man responsible for the BRI at the top of China's government. Then, after this intense four-day forum, including flights back and forth across northern China, there began to be a palpable sense of inspiration and excitement from many of the participants.

On leaving the Great Hall, and after reiterated calls to cover this grand global project, with increasing confidence and magnanimity by China's political leaders, combined with the

A meeting in the Great Hall of the People with Zhang Gaoli, the first-ranked Vice Premier of the People's Republic of China.

accumulated awe at China's modernization as seen throughout Beijing, and in light of myriad reflections on the life and times of the ancient Silk Road—there came a sense of wonder.

A sense, perhaps not fully conscious for most, that the world was clearly headed in a new direction—a direction no longer based on the mistakes of the past, a new direction, based on global cooperation towards our shared destiny.

And perhaps, by the end of this conference, even the most cynical of the participants would agree, that even if it is not perfect, it is a good direction. It is the New Silk Road worth taking!

The author was also a participant in the inauguration of the People's Daily*'s new Center for International Studies, to act as a foreign adviser for the next three years. Fourteen participants were selected from the U.K., France, Germany, Holland, Israel, India, Canada, the United States, Australia, Japan, Russia, and Thailand.*

Headquarters building of the China Global Television Network (CGTN).

The Choice Before Germany and Europe

Helga Zepp-LaRouche addressed the convention of the German political party she founded and leads, "Civil Rights Movement Solidarity," or BüSo, on Sept. 17, just one week before the German national elections, in which she headed its slate of candidates in Berlin. Her address has been translated and edited, and the title above and subheads have been added.

Dear BüSo members, honored ladies and gentlemen, dear guests,

This is already a memorable moment in history. I think we have a real problem in this election campaign, if you know what's going on in the world (and I think you all know a lot about it, because you are in contact with the BüSo), and you compare it to the "virtual reality" in Germany, as presented by the media and the so-called established, acknowledged parties, one might almost think that there are two perfectly parallel universes, where one has almost nothing to do with the other.

The good news is, of course, that there is only one universe. Therefore, this condition we have in Germany is temporary and will surely disappear.

I would like to begin by expressing my deep optimism that I think that the chances that the cause of humanity will prevail, in a relatively short time, are extremely good: the victory of mankind. By this I mean a new epoch in the history of mankind, much more in accordance with man's character than that which nowadays presents itself with the trans-Atlantic axiomatics; This is absolutely within reach, and I hope I will be able to explain it to you in such a way that perhaps by the end of my speech, you will share my optimism.

For if the situation is viewed only from Germany—and most of our citizens really only view the world from within the parameters of how it appears in Germany (which is, however, in absolute, diametrical opposition to the historical processes which are developing at this moment)—if the information which can be obtained from the BüSo were gone from our website and our newspaper, and all that were available to us were what the ordinary citizen learns from the mass media, and from the debates, or the so-called "duels" between [leading candidates] Merkel and Schulz, or even other politicians, which is what they are doing in the election campaign: this is actually largely a collection of *Fake News*, of false information that creates a completely wrong picture of the world.

For example, almost everything, or more precisely, 98%, of what the ARD (Germany's Association of

BüSo organizers bringing reality to members of the German population.

Public Broadcasting) says about President Trump is negative. And most of it has always a so-called "spin," where, even if they report a fact occasionally, there is always a negative implication. The same is true for President Putin, who is Satan incarnate, if the media is to be believed, and one is surprised that he is not portrayed with cloven hooves and breathing sulfur. Of course, the coverage of China is primarily negative; there is currently a giant explosion of so-called "China bashing." The biggest fake news of all, of course, is what the EU itself says about its own economic condition.

In other words, if one is restricted to such sources of information—unless the citizen is truly truth-loving and researches all the international press resources, and has an idea of where the important processes are taking place and is looking specifically for that information— he or she has almost no chance of getting a coherent picture.

For example, when we have information tables on the streets, we frequently encounter people here and there who have come to a definite conclusion, but even that is often like the famous Italian minestrone, the vegetable soup with radishes, potatoes, cucumbers and all sorts of other vegetables, which is to say it is not cohesive—and that is really a difficult problem.

In spite of all this, even statistics show that in Germany only 42% of the people are satisfied with the course of events, with government policy. This is roughly the same as in America. By contrast, in China, 87% of people are happy about the direction the Chinese government has taken.

The biggest problem—and this is the main problem we in BüSo have in this election campaign, where we have to fight against such obstacles—is that our citizens are saddled with a fully controlled public opinion which is policed by the media; a control of information that carefully ensures that the really important topics are not discussed, and that their existence is not known at all. Germany today, to put it mildly, is less well informed than Dresden was at the time of the GDR [the former communist East Germany], when at that time Dresden was known as the "Valley of the Clueless." As a result, there is no debate, no discussion among citizens, among institutions in Germany—less than in any other country I know of.

What does the future actually hold for Germany? What is the role of Germany in the community of nations in this world? What is the perspective for the future? Where do we want Germany to be in 50 or 100 years?

Juncker's Absurdistan

If you listen to the recent speech by EU President Juncker on the so-called situation of the European Union, then you think you are not in Germany, but in Absurdistan. Because what Juncker said has nothing to do with reality! Juncker obviously has zero idea that the EU's reputation has suffered enormously worldwide. It is by no means the case that the EU serves as a model for the integration of other groups of states, as was earlier the case, for groupings such as the African Union, ASEAN or MERCOSUR. That time is long past, and lately the EU has shown its true face in the treatment of refugees. The attempt to organize detention camps in dictatorial states, and to use Frontex, the EU coast guard and border agency, to repel refugees, has called into question every claim to represent human values, Western values, and even democracy, before the eyes of the whole world.

This has not yet found any entry—not even a glimmer—in the thinking of Juncker, who instead says all EU members should enter the Euro currency zone. This is a completely absurd demand. Recall once again what the EU directed against the countries of southern Europe—Greece, where the banking policy has ruined one-third of the European economy; similarly in Italy, Spain, and Portugal, where, ultimately, the cost-cutting measures have only led to the result that 97% of the so-called rescue money that was supposedly given to Greece, flowed right through to the European banks, while Greece remains really desperate, except for the latest developments in cooperation with China. This procedure is now about to be repeated with Bulgaria, Romania, and with other EU members not yet in the Eurozone. This is a completely absurd demand.

Then there's Juncker's idea that the future Europe should have a European finance minister, who is likely to pick the pockets of the citizens even better than Mr. [European Central Bank President Mario] Draghi has done with the ECB so far. That is an absolutely crazy idea. The zero-interest rate policy of the ECB has significantly attacked, *de facto*, savings deposits and pension claims, and this is, of course, a creeping expropriation of the savers and pensioners. And a continuation of this zero-interest policy is completely impossible, in the long term anyway.

But perhaps the most idiotic aspect of what Juncker

proposes, at the request of the Ministers for Economic Affairs of Italy, France, and Germany, is that the EU should set up a mechanism that can block Chinese investments in Germany, in so far as they go into infrastructure and energy areas, or into technologically sensitive areas.

If you know the outlook for the world at the moment, and the state of the trans-Atlantic financial system, and that the only hope is cooperation with China, then you can only say that Juncker's proposals are absolutely self-destructive, and demonstrate an incredible arrogance, because the German economy is by no means in such a shining state as a result of contrary political directions.

One consequence is the so-called "energy turn" (*Energiewende*), the exit from nuclear power, without having a real alternative. This policy has led to a rise in the price of energy and a huge increase in electricity prices, which in turn has led to the departure of energy-intensive companies. This is basically cutting off the branch you are sitting on.

The problem that we have in this *Bundestag* [parliamentary] election is therefore: How should citizens make a responsible choice as to the future of Germany? The citizens are the sovereigns, but how are they to be able to, or how can they determine the right choice, and why is it, from the point of view of history, that it is a truly catastrophic prospect that Ms. Merkel is to be Chancellor for another four years?

It would be equally stomach-turning to imagine a Federal Chancellor Schulz [the SPD candidate]. Unfortunately the other parties provide no alternative. Look at the electoral slogans of these parties. You will find a series of speech-bubbles and empty terms: "Social justice." How is this even possible with this European Union? Or from the Christian Democratic Union [party]—"For a Germany in which we live well." That's nice, but how is that to be done? And when you slowly melt the term on the tongue, it has an implicit, unspoken, anti-foreigner connotation—not pronounced, but it flows seamlessly in that direction.

Or then, really brilliant: "New Thinking." That's from the Free Democratic Party. This is always good; one should always think anew every day; but it is contentless. It is interesting that the [public employees'

The European Commission, under President Jean-Claude Juncker, directed a ruinous banking policy against the economies of Italy, Spain, Portugal, and Greece. Below, an anti-austerity demonstration in Greece.

cc:flickr.com/photos/eppofficial/

cc:flickr.com/photos/eppofficial/

union] VERDI and various other organizations have recently filed a complaint against the ARD public broadcaster at the Broadcasting Council, because they have calculated that the FDP has received just as much broadcasting time on several topics as all other parties combined. So there is a clear preference, of hoisting the FDP into the *Bundestag*, at any cost, as the representative of this neo-liberal, monetarist economic policy.

I must say, in honor of Herr Lindner [the FDP chairman], that he has done something right. He has demanded that Germany must improve her relations with Russia, but that was his only idea—which, of course, is not so terribly new.

Then: "The future needs new ideas. And one who is able to put them through." That is Herr Schulz. The question is, of course, what is the content? What is the vision? Where is the text?

The Really Crucial Issues

What are the real issues? The most important is war and peace. It should be clear to everyone that in the age of thermonuclear weapons, peace must be our most important concern. If we do not achieve world peace, the existence of mankind is no longer guaranteed. If nuclear weapons are ever used, the logic of the strategies is that *all* nuclear weapons are used. There is relevant literature: armaments expert Theodore Postol and others have argued in detail as to why there is a fundamental difference between the use of thermonuclear weapons and conventional weapons.

The second issue is equally existential. We are on the brink of a new financial crisis which, if not prevented, will be much worse than that of 2008. And since all the tools of the so-called "toolbox" of the central banks have been exhausted, such a crash must lead to absolute chaos. Thus, a new financial crash, or alternatively, a new, just global economic order, is the second most important issue.

There is a third issue. Shall we remain in the old paradigm of the trans-Atlantic neo-cons with their wars of intervention that created the refugee crisis, the geopolitical confrontation with Russia and China, and the gap between rich and poor? Or shall we participate in the creation of a new paradigm in which we overcome geopolitics with the New Silk Road, or as President Xi Jinping has said: Let us take the leap away from geopolitics to a new paradigm of humanity and the common goals of humanity?

Then a fourth issue: the image of Man. There is no debate in this election about the image of Man. The question is, is man only a parasite that pollutes the environment, and the fewer people there are, the better? This is essentially what one hears in brainless conversation. Are there no thoughts about anything nowadays? Or is mankind the only known creative species, that, through his continued scientific and technological progress, is able to investigate the laws of the universe more and more, and thereby improve the bases of life for the whole species?

These are just the most important topics—I could add others.

With regard to war and peace—how is that to be seen? It should be absolutely clear to everyone that world peace can only be maintained if Russia, China and the U.S.A. co-operate. And, of course, Europe—

but Europe is not so important in this case. If the greatest nuclear powers Russia, the U.S.A., and China, do not find a common denominator, and instead continue to the brink of armed confrontation over geopolitical conflicts, in the Middle East, in Korea, or Ukraine, then it is only a matter of time until this goes terribly wrong. That is why what the media reports about these issues is actually not just outrageous, but borders on the criminal. If you believe the media, cooperation and understanding between the U.S., Russia, and China is absolutely impossible.

Why? Because if what the media say is true, and President Trump is simply incompetent, put into power by Putin, and a racist, and that it is better to impeach him today than tomorrow—if all this is true, then it is indeed hopeless.

But in reality, this is Fake News. You do not have to be a fan of President Trump to say: The American citizens who voted for him—that's about half—do not see him as a racist. He is not a racist. He may not have been trained by Baron von Knigge [The German author of what is considered to be an authoritative guide to behavior, politeness, and etiquette—ed.], but he has quite a few advantages that make him seem to be the candidate preferred by half the American population: He wants to stop the interventionist wars that Bush, Obama and Hillary Clinton stood for, and he promised in the election campaign that he would improve relations with Russia.

That is why this whole "Russia-gate" was set up against him, which has now collapsed, because it is perfectly clear that the whole thing was an invention of the British empire. There was no Russian "hacking" of the computers of Hillary Clinton. It was an inside job, done precisely with the idea of blaming Russia for it. Hillary Clinton has not come to terms with the fact that she lost; she has just published a new book in which she asks what happened, and blames everyone except her own inability to respond to the needs of the voters. And meanwhile, this "Russia-gate" has just fallen apart because a group of former intelligence operatives has provided forensic evidence that, for technical reasons, there could have been no hacking.

The Real Situation

The reality, however, is, that despite all the attacks by the neo-cons and the media on Trump, there has now been an at least some instances of excellent cooperation between America and Russia in the case of Syria, where

Syrian refugees in the Kurdistan Region of Iraq load their luggage on to a boat on the Tigris River to return home.

five de-escalation zones have just been put into operation; ISIS is as good as defeated as a result. It has no geographical base except for the most minimal niches, and instead there is cooperation between the U.S.A. and Russia. As a result, 600,000 refugees have already returned to their homes, and the massive reconstruction of Syria and Iraq is now beginning. There was just a big conference on this in Damascus, where there was a division of labor between Russia, which will supply the energy; China, which will build the infrastructure; Iran, which will build industrial parks; and all other nations will be invited to participate.

Did you read about it in the [big German dailies] *Frankfurter Allgemeine Zeitung* or in the *Bildzeitung*? I doubt it very strongly, for although I look at them every day, I have not seen it.

More problematic, of course, is the situation in North Korea, where a dispute is still taking place in the Trump administration between the neo-cons in the Republican Party and Trump, which unfortunately has led to a situation where the Pentagon is sticking with the policy of Bush and Obama, which terminated the earlier, very positive policy launched under South Korean President Kim Dae-jung, who set in motion the "Sunshine Policy" where South Korean and North Korean engineers and workers worked together with Russians in the construction of industrial zones in North Korea.

This effort was sabotaged by Bush and Cheney at the time, and in its place they substituted the encirclement policy against China and Russia. Unfortunately this is still the policy, reflected by the installation of the THAAD missiles in South Korea. But Russia and China have both demanded a workable solution, consisting of a double-freeze: North Korea conducts no more nuclear tests, and no more missile tests, and the U.S.A. and South Korea conduct no more military maneuvers. This was wrecked by the United States and South Korea. Kim Jong-un, who has observed the situation carefully, said recently that the only chance he has to survive personally, is to make North Korea a full nuclear power—with long-range missiles and nuclear warheads—because in his eyes, that is his only chance to avert a fate like that of Saddam Hussein or Muammar Gaddafi.

Russia and China have the policy that the only way a solution to the North Korean crisis can be found is

The Rason-Russia railway link, constructed by North and South Koreans along with Russians during the "Sunshine Policy" period between North and South Korea, extended a standard gauge rail line from Russia to Rajin Port in North Korea.

State Department

U.S. Assistant Secretary of State Victoria Nuland and U.S. Ambassador to Ukraine Geoffrey Pyatt (left), with Ukrainian President-elect Petro Poroshenko (right) in Warsaw, June 4, 2014.

with the diplomatic path, and that is a demand that we emphatically, also in the U.S.A., have made our main theme. For it is not the case that China holds the key to the Korean crisis, but rather the U.S.A. The U.S.A. needs to change its policies, and then the Korean conflict can be solved simply by diplomatic negotiations.

Equally problematic is the situation in Ukraine, which is estimated by some Russian observers to be perhaps even more dangerous than North Korea. This is due to the fact that Russia is not the only one that triggered this crisis.

The narrative you read in the media is that it was the occupation of the Crimea by Russia which caused the crisis. This is absolutely absurd. The crisis in Ukraine began, in 1997, when the neo-cons in Washington committed themselves to the doctrine of the Project for a New American Century, whose idea was that the world must become unipolar, and that all governments which oppose this unipolar world are to be removed by means of "color revolutions," by regime changes, or by interventionist warfare. During the collapse of the Soviet Union, promises were made to Gorbachov and others that NATO would never extend its troops to the borders of Russia. While these promises were being made, a different policy was already in place, as Jack Matlock, who was then Ambassador in Moscow, very clearly said.

Former Chancellor Helmut Schmidt put the date of the beginning of the Ukraine crisis at 1992, with the Maastricht Treaty, because that was the point where the

decision was made to expand the EU eastwards—without any limits!

Robert Cooper, a British diplomat and advisor currently serving as a Special Advisor to the European Commission with regard to Myanmar, once said that the EU is the greatest imperial expansion in history, and without end; so the states are to be integrated endlessly. That was why Victoria Nuland could boast that the U.S. State Department alone had spent $5 billion on NGOs in Ukraine, which led to the Orange Revolution in 2004, and then to the attempt to incorporate Ukraine into the EU, to which President Viktor Yanukovych would not agree at the EU summit in Vilnius; and then to the Maidan, where the NGOs combined with the fascists to overthrow the legitimately elected government. The German government played an absolutely active part. The Konrad Adenauer Foundation, like the State Department, got in on the act with Wladimir Klitschko, the former boxer; then Victoria Nuland, who in the famous telephone call with the four-letter word against the EU, announced that she wanted to have "Yats" [Arseniy Yatsenyuk] take over as Prime Minister, as he soon did.

When one considers all of this, the sham of the so-called "narrative," with respect to the Ukraine crisis, is absolutely scandalous. And it is also scandalous when, in this tradition, Merkel, through the EU, extended sanctions against Russia, until at least March 2018, and possibly even until September. This is diametrically opposed to German interests.

New Financial Crisis?

Now to the third theme: new financial crisis or equitable new world economic order. We are sitting on an absolute powder keg. On the very day that Mr. Juncker announced how wonderful the economic situation in Europe is, the Adam Smith Institute published a report—the Adam Smith Institute, a neo-liberal think-tank based in Britain, published a report stating that the next financial crisis is an accident waiting to happen, simply because the situation is so completely tense.

At the same time, the European Financial Market Authority issued a warning that the next crisis is imminent. The reasons for this are the internal tensions in the U.S.A., which they say is the danger of civil war, and geopolitical crises.

Commodity speculation: Houston oil traders' office.

The ECB has simply ignored the whole issue of Level 3 derivatives—these are the derivatives that do not even have a market price because they are virtually unsalable—with the argument that each major bank has its own model, its own algorithm which it uses to assign value, and that the ECB has no competence to investigate this. You can toss their assurances straight into the trash bin, because these stress tests simply did not take place.

In these circumstances, a "more of the same" policy, as especially Ms. Merkel and for that matter also Schulz promote, is really irresponsible. For if the new financial crash occurs, since the "tools" have already been used, and the zero-interest policy has already taken place, the collapse into chaos and its consequences will be absolutely unimaginable.

In the meantime, even the mass media—*Der Spiegel*, *Die Welt* and others—have warned that the next financial crisis is only a matter of a short time from now. The former Italian Finance and Economics Minister, Giulio Tremonti, has said that the situation is the same as between the two world wars. The "First World War" was in 2008, then comes an interregnum, where the real causes that led to the First World War (the 2008 crisis) are not resolved, so they are discharged in the "Second World War"—the imminent next financial crisis that will surely come on if no countermeasures are deployed.

The debt of governments, companies, student loans, and auto loans are on average 40-80% worse than 2008. Why? Instead of ending the excessive derivative speculation, and ending proprietary trading, what have the central banks done? They have gone for zero-interest policies, money printing, and rescue packages; the ECB has pumped 80 billion Euros a year into the financial system, an enormous amount of liquidity. However, this did not mean that companies invested in real investments, but rather in the buying up their own stock shares, which of course looks excellent on the books — the stock market profits go up, the shares are elevated— while at the same time the companies are so indebted that Draghi simply does not dare to raise the interest rate even a quarter of a percentage point, because then the entire house of cards would collapse. All the so-called "stress tests" are fictions.

The Mood in the U.S.A. is Changing

That is why what you hear from the media is irresponsible—above all, because the prospects for a solution are not discussed. In contrast to the way Trump is depicted, what you have never heard from the media has been a change in his thinking as a result of the unusual series of natural catastrophes, namely the hurricanes, where Hurricane Harvey destroyed Texas and caused a total damage estimated at least $200 billion; also in Florida and the other southern states—just as we have some recollection in Germany of such flood catastrophes. When men are threatened by such catastrophes, it is the natural tendency of humans that their humanity comes to the fore. And in the case of Texas and Florida, this has resulted in an unprecedented outpouring of aid and solidarity, from volunteers who have flown there, and from neighbors who have helped one another. And this has changed the poisonous climate previously produced by the media and the Democrats against Trump, who were recently demanding his immediate impeachment. And now, leading Democrats like Chuck Schumer, Nancy Pelosi and Diane Feinstein have met with Trump and, for example, have agreed upon emergency aid for the flood victims. Several leading Democrats have said that it is no longer good enough to be simply against Trump. Because they have noticed that that has not helped them at all. Trump won some by-elections, because the population is not swallowing it. Americans are not so stupid as to not notice when they are presented with one fairy-tale after another. That is why the Democrats have already turned their backs on "tactical calculations," and are now looking for a dialogue with Trump, which is of course a huge blow to the neocon leaders in the Republican Party.

This is very important. Yesterday [September 16] Trump, in his weekly radio address, appealed to all Americans to rebuild the country—and basically a spirit of the good Samaritan now prevails, where it doesn't matter whether someone is Republican or Democrat.

Yesterday there was a large demonstration in Washington,

Donald Trump speeches & press conference

President Trump meeting with GOP Senate Majority Leader Mitch McConnell (on couch, left), Democratic Party Senator Chuck Schumer, and House Minority Leader Nancy Pelosi, Sept. 6, 2017.

where our people had a great deal of influence. Now we really have the prerequisites to bring the Four Laws proposed by Lyndon LaRouche into the debate: Glass-Steagall, the banking separation system that Trump promised in the election campaign; a return to the policy of Alexander Hamilton, which Trump also promised; a national bank like Hamilton's first Bank of the United States; a credit system; and a rebuilding of the U.S.A.

For many people, this may seem to be absolutely unimaginable, but those of you who have been in the United States lately, know the infrastructure is in a worse state than in the final phase of the DDR [German Democratic Republic, the former East Germany]. In the freeways, they have potholes. I would definitely not recommend driving a Fiat 500, because the chances are relatively good that you will be swallowed up. The subways in New York have decayed, they are 100 years old, there are fires and derailments of trains. There are only 250 km of high speed rail track in the U.S.A. Two hundred fifty km! And with a maximum speed of only 90 miles per hour. You have to imagine this; China now has 20,000 km of high speed rail track on which the trains go at 200 mph and are much better than the ICEs in Germany.

The U.S.A. Must Work with China

The U.S.A. is therefore in such an urgent need of infrastructure investment, that we have launched a huge campaign for China and the United States to work together. China has already said that the United States needs $8 trillion in infrastructure investment, and is willing to cooperate there. This is the only chance America has. If Trump does not implement Glass-Steagall and the full program of the "Four Laws," then he will not get any funding for it. Neither can the budget be endlessly increased, nor new debts taken; the United States has already $20 trillion in government debt, an absolute absurdity, while we are pointing out that China has $1.4 trillion in U.S. government bonds as currency reserves, and could use these reserves sensibly by investing in building infrastructure in the U.S.A.

Contrary to what you hear in the media, such investments are not out of the question. The good news is that Trump is not the crazy man the media depict him to be. He has developed a very good line of communication to Xi Jinping. Since their summit at Mar-a-Lago in April, they have constantly telephoned each other, even during the ongoing Korean crisis. They had a very good meeting in Hamburg at the G20 summit, and right now, U.S. Secretary of State Rex Tillerson and Yang Jiechi, the State Councilor of China (the number three position in the goverment) are preparing a state visit for Trump, probably to take place at the end of November during the ASEAN meeting, and there is a good chance that the anti-geopolitical perspective will take a good step forward.

The Dynamics of the New Silk Road

That is to say, the possibility that there can be cooperation between Russia, the U.S.A. and China is a potential that absolutely exists. And if you read *Forbes* magazine—that's the only coverage. If you listen to the rest of the media, you may hear only one per cent positive coverage. Nonetheless, there is a completely new dynamic with the New Silk Road. The new paradigm, which the BüSo wants to put on the agenda, already exists, and has so for a long time. It is what we have widely promoted since the inception of the BüSo, but I would say even longer by my husband and myself, 40 years—in the case of my husband even over 50 years. This is going to happen. There is a new world economic order coming that is completely different from anything you know in Germany or even in Europe.

Xi Jinping proposed to the world a New Silk Road in 2013, only four years ago. But in these four years an enormous dynamic has developed, and an infrastructure and economic development program is underway worldwide which is already twelve times or even twenty times the size of the Marshall Plan after the Second World War.

The fact that this is not discussed here in the media borders on the criminal, because if Germans knew that there was such a development, and they could see the options and opportunities for Germany in this program, the mood would be much better.

I would say that the very fact that we are absolutely clear with regard to the responsibility of the neocons, the parties and the media, is probably the reason why, in this election campaign or otherwise, they have tried to cast any contact that we have with the public in a negative light—such as this impudent broadcast on the ARD about the so-called small parties—because they can not bear to have people know about this perspective at all.

The New Silk Road now involves over 70 nations, all of Eurasia or nearly all of Eurasia. Latin America is covered by it, as is Africa. It is a completely new concept, which Xi Jinping always calls the "community for the future of mankind." And Xi Jinping has shown a tremendous personal commitment to the new world order. He has made 28 state visits, travelling to 56 states on five continents, creating optimism everywhere, especially in developing countries, which is absolutely unprecedented.

But this is not what the media report, claiming instead that it is only the Chinese drive for power, the power fantasies of China, that wants to buy the whole world, and which supposedly wants to replace Anglo-American imperialism with a Chinese imperialism. It is really extremely important that we oppose this negative propaganda—which is what it is.

Cui Tiankai, the Chinese ambassador to Washington, recently delivered a speech in New York, in which he said he had looked through history, and that there were 16 instances in which an ascending power overtook the dominant power. In 12 of these 16 cases, it came to war, and in four cases the rising power simply overtook the dominant power. He said that China does not want to follow the twelve examples where war came—nor even the four, where China would simply replace the dominance of the U.S.A., but instead prefers a completely new model of cooperation, mutual respect for sovereignty, non-intervention, and the acceptance of the social model of the other, where one does not try to impose on the other its own model of so-called human rights or so-called democracy, by imposing so-called Western values—or for that matter Chinese values or Russian values, but rather, to seek mutual advantage in a win-win cooperation.

That is truly inspiring. I know that Europeans have great difficulties in recognizing this. For, above all, when one is accustomed to the policies we have here, one automatically projects those policies onto others. If the media here peddle the line that China has only geopolitical intentions—it is rather that it is the local media that have geopolitical intentions. If you hear someone retail the nonsense that China only wants to carry out its interests at the expense of others, that's because that's the policy here. How can you imagine that there could be a country or a political leader who has the common good in mind? That's why people have so much trouble.

China's Economic Miracle

One must simply see: The Chinese model is the greatest example of an economic miracle in history. I would even say it is better and more inspiring than the German economic miracle after the Second World War. And I am speaking with real authority, because in contrast to the China experts in the media—I would say, everyone—I was in China in 1971. I do not think one of these people can claim that, but I was on a trip in 1971 that took me to Africa and Asia, and I spent about three months in China. I got there on a freighter which, while undergoing renovations in Shanghai, allowed me the opportunity to travel around Shanghai, to Tianjin and to Beijing.

Deng Xiaoping (center) and his wife Zhuo Lin (right of him) being briefed by Johnson Space Center director Christopher C. Kraft (right front) on Feb. 2, 1979.

I can assure you that China at that time was in an absolutely catastrophic state. The people were unhappy. I was still very young. Many tearful people told me in German or English (in Qingdao and Shanghai, many people spoke either German or English), stories about the Red Guards tearing people out of their beds at night, and sending them to work in the fields. The few people who had a developed profession, like a pilot or an engineer, were sent to the countryside, allegedly for "petty bourgeois corruption." The Red Guards had all the works of art painted red. In Beijing at the Summer Palace, I saw the wonderful arcades all covered in red. It was a period that Chinese today describe as the low point in their history, roughly comparable to the twelve years of National Socialism in Germany. One could say that that was the low point in Germany. This was a time when Confucianism was attacked.

And then came the change. The "Gang of Four" was finally defeated after the death of Mao Zedong, and Deng Xiaoping introduced the first economic reforms. There was a relatively fast economic improvement. At that time, mistakes were made; China accepted the role of being the land of cheap manufacturing, the environment was damaged, the ground water was spoiled, the air was polluted, and there were bad factories. But then things progressed relatively quickly, at least on the east coast and in the south of China. And then, especially in the last 30 years, the Chinese economic miracle came, which has really led to the biggest contribution by China to the improvement of human rights by any country.

And this the ARD did not mention in their interview with me, which took about half an hour, out of which they took only one sentence, namely the question: "Are there any human rights violations in China?" And I said, "No," and then they cut it off. The rest of my sentence was, "the reason is that China has liberated 700 million people from the deepest poverty, and poverty is one of the biggest human rights violations, and that is why China has an excellent record, so it is an excellent success story." The ARD, of course, did not report this, and at the end of the interview, they brought in an agent provocateur who said the BüSo supported dictatorships like China and Russia. This is really a prime example of how to turn something around completely.

But the conditions of the 1970s and 1980s are not the reality in China today. Today there is a profound optimism in the Chinese people, and a large middle

The Three Gorges Dam on the Yangtze River, China.

China's Experimental Advanced Superconducting Tokamak (EAST) reactor.

I'm asked again and again: "Why do you still do this when you have so few electoral successes and you are so ignored?" I do not see it that way. I tend to see that our ideas and our efforts are effective everywhere in the world, and it is only a matter of time before this is recognized and changed in Germany. (Applause.)

50 Years of Commitment

I'll take you through the stages again, because perhaps this is not known to everyone in detail.

My husband, already in 1975, was invited to Iraq, to the Baath Party celebrations, and met there many "Third World" leaders from the Non-Aligned Movement, and then came back and held press conferences in Bonn and Milan, saying: "The IMF is bankrupt, morally and practically, because it blocks the development of the Third World through conditionalities."

The IMF has always demanded that the priority must be the repayment of debts rather than investments in infrastructure or social systems. My husband then proposed the International Development Bank (IDB), the idea that a new credit mechanism would be needed, through which the industrialized countries would finance DM400 billion every year of technology transfer to the Third World.

This was an absolutely correct proposal, and we discussed it for a whole year with embassies from Third World countries or where we had contacts in the affected countries, such as India and elsewhere; and a year later the Non-Aligned Movement in its summit in Sri Lanka published a resolution for a just new world economic order, almost identical in text to what was written in the IDB proposal.

At that time, I think, 70 nations supported the resolution, and I called the head of the DPA [German government press agency] service and asked him, "When are you going to report that? The majority of humanity has just decided on a just new world economic order!"

He replied "Oh, this is not newsworthy, we won't carry it." I said, "What? That's three-quarters of humanity, and you do not consider it worth reporting?" And he says, "No, that's not our topic."

class of about 900 million, a huge market for Europe and the U.S.A., potentially, and that is why this policy of "China bashing" is like sawing off the branch on which you're sitting. China plans to overcome the last four percent of poverty by 2020, especially in rural areas. China has committed itself to helping to overcome poverty all over the world, and above all, China has a completely different approach. They rely on the brilliance of their citizens, the Confucian idea of lifelong learning. They now have 2,000 students enrolled in doctoral programs for nuclear fusion; they have the world's most advanced fusion energy experiment. And they will connect all major cities by high-speed railways by 2020. In problem regions, i.e., where cities are too large, as in the case of Beijing—take the region of Beijing-Hebei-Tianjin—they are building entirely new cities, in order to reduce the congestion, along with environmentally friendly industries. So they are acting quite differently from the West.

Our connection with this New Silk Road is really an extremely close one. And this is something that the media control will not be able to change. One can say, this is what Lyndon LaRouche, my husband, and I and our movement have campaigned for worldwide, for 30, 40, 50 years—in the case of my husband, certainly 50 years. For a long time these were only ideas like utopias, only blueprints, only programmatic conceptions. Now that China,—which is probably already the strongest economic power, which is making great strides—has taken it up, it is no longer just a utopian dream.

Indira Ghandi at the National Press Club, Washington, D.C., July 30, 1982.

Mexican President José López Portillo, Feb. 14, 1977.

1989: LaRouche's Proposed European 'Productive Triangle' Rail Development

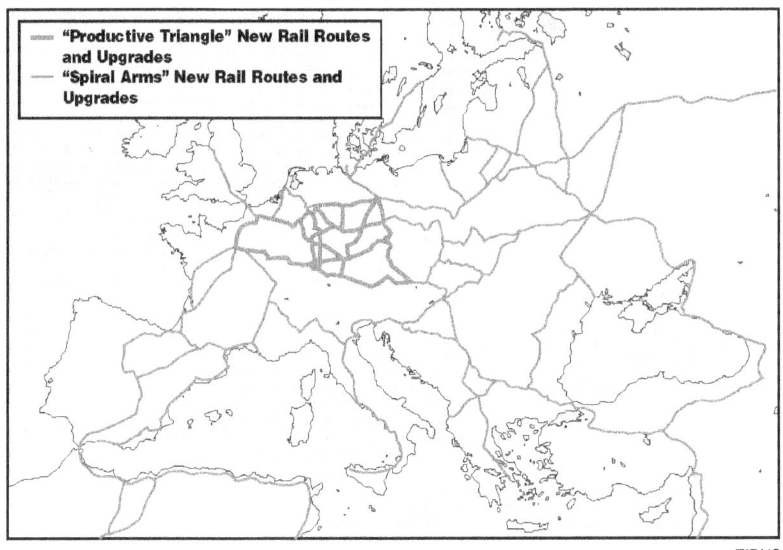

Then, of course, there was a huge counter-reaction—Sri Lankan Prime Minister Sirimavo Bandaranaike, Indian Prime Minister Indira Gandhi, and Pakistan Prime Minister Zulfikar Ali Bhutto were all either killed or destabilized, so this whole movement once again suffered a setback. But we have always worked on these things. My husband also proposed the Oasis Plan in 1975, for the development of the Middle East, through the creation of new water resources to combat the deserts. This Oasis Plan was absolutely under discussion, on many occasions.

At the end of the 1970s, we worked with Prime Minister Indira Gandhi on a 40-year development plan for India. We continued this work with her son Rajiv Gandhi. Both were murdered, and this development plan has not been brought to fruition.

We worked on a 50-year development plan for the Pacific Basin. We set up conferences, including in Thailand for the Kra Kanal, in 1984. We worked with Mexican President José López Portillo on an integration plan for Latin America, which we called "Operation Juarez."

Through all these years, we have presented very concrete development plans, and we have worked together with the governments of the countries.

We responded to the collapse of the Soviet Union in 1991 with the program of the Eurasian Land-Bridge. In 1984, my husband forecast that the Soviet Union would collapse if it stayed with its economic policy at that time, rejecting the Strategic Defense Initiative.

At that time there was no one else who had said that the Soviet Union would cease to exist. But as we had already correctly assessed it, we presented a plan for the reunification of Germany—a year before it happened—a plan for the development of the COMECON countries, which was the "Productive Triangle Paris-Berlin-Vienna." And when the Soviet Union did disband in 1991, we simply extended the plan, by saying that the industrial and population centers of Europe must be connected with those in Asia through infrastructure corridors. We proposed this program to all the governments of Eurasia.

The only government that responded was China. But it took over two years for our proposal to be finally implemented in 1996, because China wanted to work with the EU. Sir Leon Brittan delayed it two and a half years, by arguing (unsuccessfully) that the financing for the Land-Bridge projects must be left in private hands.

In 1996, at a big conference in Beijing on the New Euro-Asia Continental Bridge, I spoke on the development of the regions along the Eurasian Land-Bridge.

Ours was the strategic long-term orientation of China however. They definitely wanted to do it at that time. But as you may recall, the Asian crisis broke out in 1997, when speculators including especially George Soros, manipulated the values of currencies downward by 80% within a week,—what Prime Minister Mahathir of Malaysia described as a crime against the Malaysian people. As a result, there followed the Russian state bankruptcy, the GKO crisis in 1998. This brought the Land-Bridge developments to a standstill, but did not deter us from continuing to campaign for it.

In 1998, I was on a very important trip through four Chinese cities, in a Russian-Chinese delegation, including Prof. Lvov and Prof. Mikhail Titarenko, the top China expert in Russia, both from the Russian Academy of Sciences, and also some top Chinese experts. The idea was to make the concept of the New Silk Road known in the regions. That is why the first conference was held in Beijing, the second in Nanjing, the third in Lianyungang, and the fourth in another place, whose name is always omitted.

That was the idea at the time, and we have organized more and more conferences since then, with our colleagues in Australia, in several African countries, in Sao Paulo where my husband became an honorary citizen of the city, in Brasilia, Rio de Janeiro, in Mexico (where López Portillo said in 1998 that "It is now necessary for the world to listen to the wise words of Lyndon LaRouche"), Beijing, many other Chinese cities, New Delhi, Mumbai, and Bangalore, as well as many European and American cities.

It has frequently been said, "This is a nice plan, but it will never be a reality, because you are too small, and it will not happen at all." But, it is happening. My fundamental optimism that we can bring about the same effect in Germany, is based on the long arc of our activity and practical experience, which teaches us that if an idea is appropriate, and if it addresses a fundamental need of mankind, it can be implemented.

Xi Jinping Realized the Proposals

When Xi Jinping prposed the New Silk Road in Kazakhstan in 2013, we were extremely happy. I think we may have opened a bottle of sparkling wine at the time and claimed this as really our victory. We very quickly updated the various studies we had done over the years, into a comprehensive report, and called it *The New Silk Road Becomes the World Land-Bridge*.

At the time we published it in 2014, it was still a utopia. But the Chinese themselves said: This is the most developed proposal, and all Chinese scholars should read this study. The Chongyang Financial Institute sent it to 1,000 think tanks and university faculties in China, with the requirement that all scholars should study it.

We translated it into Arabic. It was presented by the Egyptian Minister of Transport in Cairo as the Egyptian policy for the Middle East and Africa. It has also appeared in German in the meantime. It will soon appear in Korean—it is already translated and is only a question of finding the right publisher. And a second edition of this World Land-Bridge study series, will also appear in a few weeks. It will be even more detailed on the development of the Middle East and Africa.

The situation now is completely changed. China has completely changed the mood in Africa within the framework of the New Silk Road. China has built a 750 km railroad from Djibouti to Addis Ababa, it is building a railway from Kenya which will eventualy go to Rwanda, and it has built many dams and industrial parks. The mood of Africans is no longer such that they think they should listen to the sermons of the European politicians, but they say: We want to be treated as equals; we want direct investments; and we want the Europeans to do the same as China.

In accordance with its philosophy, China has invited all countries to participate. It does not just want to establish its own interests in Africa. Xi Jinping has made concrete offers of cooperation to to Merkel and others, to participate.

Transaqua Will Transform Africa

An essential aspect of our World Land-Bridge study, which we have been actively presenting at conferences since at least the beginning of the 1990s, is the Transaqua program. Transaqua is a concept that will totally change Africa because it brings about 3-4% of the water from the Congo tributaries at a height of 500 m through a channel system traversing twelve states to Lake Chad. Lake Chad is now shrunk to less than 10% of its original volume, which of course has exacerbated conditions of life and poverty in the region, in the Sahel zone, and has paved the way for terrorist organizations such as Boko Haram.

The Transaqua program would create an inland navigation system, which would allow inland navigation among twelve neighboring countries, and would provide incredible amounts of water for irrigation of agricultural land; it would increase food production massively; it would generate hydroelectric power for all twelve states; it would facilitate the development of other infrastructure; and when implemented, it will be the largest infrastructure program in history.

There is now a contract for this program between the Chinese government and the Italian government, and between Bonifica—the company that developed this plan—and the Chinese company PowerChina.

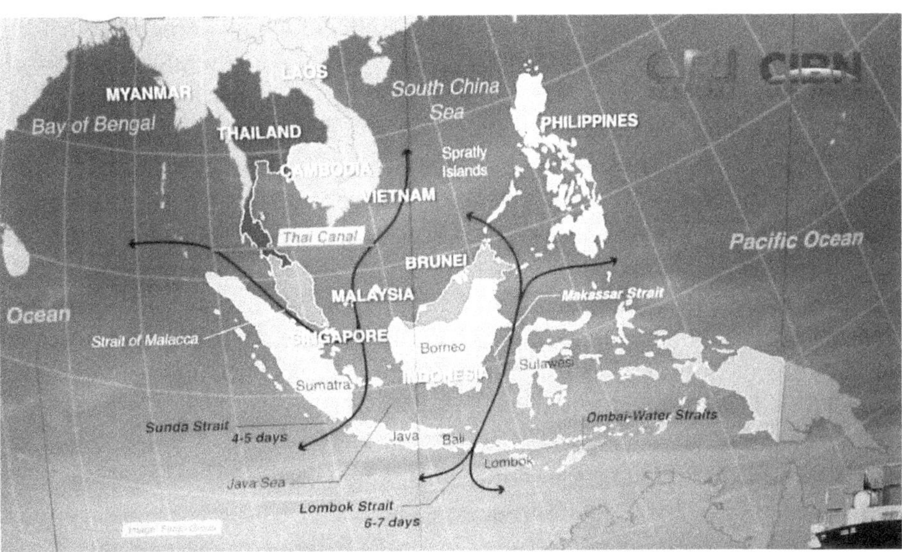

Map showing the strategic location, for shipping, of the Thai (Kra) Canal.

PowerChina is experienced in infrastructure; it built the Three Gorges Dam which has forever tamed the Yangtze River, whose flooding used to take thousands of lives every few years. Flood catastrophes will no longer take place there. This is the company, together with Bonifica, that wants to build Transaqua.

Just to emphasize our involvement: *People's Daily* had a long article about Transaqua a few weeks ago, in which they credit the LaRouche organization, *EIR*, and the Schiller Institute for bringing about the connection between China and Italy.

Our Ideas Will Prevail

This is all really very good. One sees in the case of Transaqua that if it is done right, our ideas will prevail. It may take 20, 30 years, sometimes even longer—as in the case of Plato or Confucius, where it took many years for their ideas to dominate, but one must believe in the *power of ideas.* Ideas are much more important than money, much more important than vote percentages, much more important than democratic majorities. What good is the most perfect democratic majority when the ideas it carries are bad and destructive?

Transaqua is just one example. Another example where our ideas are now concrete, is in the reconstruction of Syria.

Some of you will know that we—as the Schiller Institute—organized a major conference in Frankfurt in 2012, where we discussed a program for the Middle East, and said that the situation can only be stabilized when all the big neighbors—Russia, China, India, Pakistan, Iran, Egypt, work together—because this is the only way to calm the situation. And this is exactly what is happening now: A collaboration of Russia, U.S.A., China—India not so much at the moment—but Iran, Pakistan and Egypt—they are all on this course. The New Silk Road is today, finally, being demanded and being built in the Middle East, making it possible to overcome the problem of refugees in the Middle East in a humane way—as well as the problem of African refugees who certainly will not want to come to an unfriendly Europe when their own home represents a future.

The third example of our ideas being realized today is the Kra Canal. The Kra Canal is a project that we have been advocating since the beginning of the 1980s. This is the idea to relieve the congestion in the Strait of Malacca, which has the largest volume of trade in the world—the greatest number of the ships pass through a strait which is very narrow, so it is overloaded, and constantly threatened by pirates. The idea is to build a channel through the Isthmus of Thailand, which then, like the Suez Canal and the Panama Canal, creates a parallel path for transport.

To this end, a conference took place in Bangkok on September 11, six days ago, where some of the speakers who were present also attended a 1984 conference at which my husband and I were present as speakers—but this time there was top participation by the royal institutions of Thailand, by top Japanese institutions, Malaysians, and Chinese. There have been many articles in the Chinese press that have said that China should absolutely be involved, and Japan absolutely as well. And, of course, it is also clear that peace is created by development.

Another place where we are directly involved is Latin America. As you may know, as a part of this operation, we have always used "Operation Juarez" for the infrastructure development of the Latin American continent, which, like Africa, did not have any infrastructure from the colonial era, to speak of. And now, through Chinese intervention, the idea of a bi-oceanic Land-Bridge, a railway connection from Brazil to Peru, and a second link from Brazil through Bolivia to Peru, is quite concrete.

Here, too, there is now a glimmer of light: At the Kra Canal conference, the European Chambers of Commerce took part—the first sign of madness fading [laughs], signs of health—and also on this bi-oceanic railway, especially the southern route, German and Swiss companies are now very keen to get involved.

This is the obvious way out for Germany, because it is in the fundamental interest of German industry, above all the German *Mittelstand* [smaller, independent businesses], to participate in all such projects. That the New Silk Road is growing all over the world, and Germany somehow remains an island that is excluded, is absurd. It will not happen. It is in the self-interest of the German *Mittlestand* to participate in these projects.

This is the leading dynamism in the world, and this is what is happening in Eastern Europe, which is taking place in the "16 + 1" states [sixteen Central and East European contries plus China]. Greece just had a great trade fair in Thessaloniki, where all the press agencies of Southern Europe were present, all of whom said, in effect: "No, what the EU says is perfect nonsense—China is not a threat; China is not buying the Port of Piraeus against Greek interests, but quite the opposite—Greece can only survive through Chinese investment." China is building a railway from Budapest to Belgrade, and the EU wants to ban it. That is absurd! The EU has done nothing for 20 years. China is not the reason why the EU is divided. It is China which has turned toward a divided Europe with offers to help.

The Chinese are very self-assured, and the Serbs are glad that China is there, the Hungarians are glad, and the Italians are glad. Spain and Portugal want to be "hubs," not just for the final phase of the Eurasian Land-Bridge in Europe, but as hubs for trade with Latin America and the Portuguese-speaking countries in Africa.

The idea that this somehow ought to be resisted is therefore completely absurd. And if you look at the enormous change that has happened in just four years—four years really is just such a trice, that is, from the point of view of history. It's really nothing. Then the idea that "Europe," the EU *status quo*, with its guidelines and crazy prescriptions, which must be preserved—it's all really ridiculous. I am, therefore, really optimistic that this EU, in the form it now exists, will end up very soon in the dustbin of history, and instead a completely different order will be hegemonic, namely the cooperation of sovereign states in the greater interests of mankind.

In other respects there are already discussions underway—if you came here by train, ICE, you would never get this idea—but elsewhere there are quite different ideas. Think of what the camel was for the old Silk Road—camels, horses, donkeys, etc.—which greatly improved the crossing of the desert and steppes. Human beings would never have been able to walk through the Taklamakan desert, the Gobi desert, or other deserts. It was the camels that made it possible.

Taking their place, in the last four years we have witnessed 40 or perhaps even more direct trains from China to Europe departing every week, from Chongqing, Chengdu, Yiwu, Lianyungang, Xi'an and various other Chinese cities, traveling to Duisburg, Hamburg, Lyons, Rotterdam, Madrid—filling all these cities with great optimism, because the railroads bring jobs again. Duisburg, for example, which had been completely run down by the deindustrialization policies, now sees itself with unique opportunities as the largest inland port of Europe and Germany.

But that's not all. Conventional railways, even if fantastic, are only for now. Already there are automated, fully air-conditioned containers for goods that are very sensitive and must survive temperature differences from +40 C in summer to –45 C in winter using climate control—containers which are remotely controlled, which are GPS-capable—these are the "camels" of the New Silk Road.

There are quite a few other ideas. For example, China and Japan are building new rapid transit systems, to soon connect Kunming, Singapore, Moscow, and Beijing. China is developing the new Fuxing railway, also a new conventional high-speed railroad, which will travel at 400 km/h. China, Japan, and the U.S.A. are already developing hyperloop systems that will allow speeds of 1,000 km/h, initially to transport goods,

Xinhua/Zhu Xiang

First direct cargo train leaving for Europe from Zhengzhou, capital of China's Henan Province.

and soon thereafter passengers. Supersonic aircraft are now also being developed, so that the entire transportation system and the connectedness of mankind will be completely transformed in the future.

To a Mankind Growing Together

The future of mankind will be different. It will be based on the idea that we are really growing together into one humanity. The idea that there are national interests that must be enforced against other national interests is a completely outdated idea that has no future. The future of mankind is the joint development of space, cooperation in the great themes that are in the interests of all people.

And it will above all lead to a different cultural understanding. Dialogue of classical cultures means that every nation will bring to life the high phase of its own culture in the way, for example, that China is having a renaissance of Confucian culture. The ideas of Confucius are what inspire Xi Jinping. Xi Jinping is a Renaissance man; he is a Confucian philosopher who develops the idea of Confucius, that every human being not only develops all his abilities evenly to a harmonious whole—which is the same idea as Friedrich Schiller, or Wilhelm von Humboldt—but also the harmonious development of families, the development of the nation as a whole and the coexistence of the nations among each other, by the fact that each nation develops all the potential that exists in it and that there is then an exchange, so that chauvinism and xenophobia and backwardness will disappear.

For China has recognized, just like the BüSo—I do not know who is more inspiring, perhaps this is an idea which must necessarily come because it simply lies in the nature of things—that contact with, and learning of the other culture leads to love when one recognizes the beauty of the other culture.

Why is it, for example, that when you go to hear an orchestra, there are more Chinese, Japanese, or Koreans in attendance than Europeans? Because in those cultures, the beauty of European classical music is recognized and not seen as a threat. Beethoven and Bach are universal poets, composers—they have long belonged to all mankind.

And it will be in the same way that the best blossoms of other cultures will also be part of our general knowledge here in Europe, as will be the case again with classical music. The beauty of Chinese painting, e.g., "literati painting," where one can see the painting—landscape or animals or people—and a poem, and the calligraphy, the beauty of the writing, where one can understand what a metaphor is—better than that in European painting, because there is no such specific match in European painting. It will also be noted that many other cultures have produced works of art which enormously enriches us as humanity.

That is why, I think, we must not only look at the next few weeks, or even only up to the *Bundestag* election, which is only a step for us—a step from which, however, we must rapidly progress.

If you ask me, "Who is going to prevail, Mr. Juncker, Mr. Draghi, Mr. Schäuble?" Then I would argue that these people belong to a defunct paradigm, which really does not exist any more. They attempt to maintain a status quo that does not correspond to the interests of mankind and has no chance of survival. The only chance that these people have is to make a 180-degree turn and accept the new paradigm.

Even though I do not think that some of these people are flexible and mobile enough, I think we'll prevail, and I think our BüSo program has put a New Silk Road and a renaissance of classical culture on the agenda, and this will determine the future of Germany. (Applause.)

Columbus' First 'Belt and Road' Inspired by Cusa

by Will Wertz

Sept. 30—As long maintained by Lyndon LaRouche, the seed crystal for today's One Belt, One Road grand design for world peace based on economic development traces itself back to Nicolaus of Cusa and his immediate collaborators: Paolo Toscanelli and Ferdinand Martin, the Canon of Lisbon, Portugal and confessor of King Alfonso V of Portugal. Together, they were responsible for organizing the first attempted maritime belt between Europe and China carried out by Christopher Columbus to complement the already existing Silk Road.

Nicholas of Cusa
(1401-1464)

Toscanelli and Martin were among the closest collaborators of Nicolaus of Cusa. In fact, they were the executors of his last will and testament. Toscanelli appears in Nicolaus of Cusa's *Dialogue on the Quadrature of the Circle* and Martin in Cusa's *On the Not-Other*. Nicolaus of Cusa had known Toscanelli since Cusanus studied law in Padua, Italy, graduating in 1424. When Cusanus traveled to Constantinople in 1437 at the behest of Pope Eugene IV, he was accompanied by Antonio Martin, the Bishop of Oporto, the brother of Ferdinand Martin, King Alfonso's confessor. The purpose of Cusanus' trip to Constantinople was to bring Greek and Russian Orthodox Church representatives back to Italy for the ecumenical Council of Florence, Italy, which started in 1439 and concluded in 1445.

Toscanelli, in a letter to Martin on June 25, 1474 (to be relayed to King Alfonso V of Portugal) reported that a Chinese Ambassador had met with Pope Eugene IV in Florence, Italy before the start of the Council of Florence. After meeting with the Pope, the Chinese Ambassador then met with Toscanelli personally.

The Chinese then had an advanced navigational capacity and conducted, under the leadership of Zheng He, seven major voyages. Two of these in 1414, and the

last voyage in 1433, sailed up the Red Sea to Jeddah, which is very close to Mecca. It is also reported that they visited Cairo, Egypt. The meeting with Pope Eugene IV in Florence is believed to have occurred soon after the 1433 visit to Cairo.[1] Such diplomatic exchanges between the Roman Catholic Church and Ming China began as early as 1371. During the reign of Yongle (1403-1424) China received a delegation from the papacy.[2]

Both the letter written by Toscanelli to Ferndinand Martin in

---

1. There are many sources which report on these two journeys, including: *Trade, Travel, and Exploration in the Middle Ages: An Encyclopedia,* which reports that in the 1414 voyage "A Chinese mission visited Mecca and continued to Egypt," and from http://factsanddetails.com/china/cat2/4sub8/itc_m45.html: "The seventh and final voyage (1431-33) was sent out by the Yongle emperor's successor, his grandson the Xuande emperor. This expedition had more than one hundred large ships and over 27,000 men, and it visited all the important ports in the South China Sea and Indian Ocean as well as Aden and Hormuz. One auxiliary voyage traveled up the Red Sea to Jidda, only a few hundred miles from the holy cities of Mecca and Medina." And, according to Wang Tai Peng, in "Zheng He and his Envoys' Visits to Cairo in 1414 and 1433," this final auxiliary voyage included seven envoys, who spoke a number of languages including Arabic and Latin. One of the purposes of this voyage was to announce "the Ming imperial edict of emperor Xuande to the Maijia Kingdom or Mecca, the Baigeda Kingdom or Baghdad, the Mosili Kingdom or Cairo, the Mulanpi Kingdom or Morocco and the Fulin Kingdom or Florence, that all of them were his subjects. According to Ming History, Egypt and Morocco were among foreign countries that had received the Chinese imperial edict and gifts but failed to send any tribute to Ming China. But Florence and Baghdad belonged to the category of foreign countries which had already paid tribute to Ming China during the reign of emperor Yongle (1403-1424)." The foreign rulers were to be presented with the Xuande astronomical calendar marking his inauguration and with charts and navigational aids to enable foreign rulers to return tribute to China.

2. In *The Papacy and Ancient China* by Tai Peng Wang, the following sources are cited: Yan Conglina: Zhuyu Zhouzi Lu [Comprehensive Record of Foreign Lands] and Zhang Xing Lang: Zhangxi Jiaotong Shiliao Huibian [Collected Historical Sources of the History of Contacts between China and the West], Vol. 1, Chapter 6, p. 315.

1474 and the letter written to Columbus in 1480 appear below.

In the letter to Martin, Toscanelli makes it clear that the Chinese were governed by "astronomers and other men skilled in the natural sciences." Then in his letter to Columbus, Toscanelli emphasizes "the most copious and good and true information from distinguished men of great learning who have come here in the [Papal] court of Rome [Florence at that time] from the said parts." These passages, considered together, suggest strongly that the Chinese knowledge of astronomy and navigation contributed to his confidence in the success of the project to reach China and India by sailing west.

Following that visit of the Chinese Ambassador to Florence, the ecumenical Council of Florence was organized with the intention of reuniting the Roman Catholic Church with the Greek and Russian Orthodox churches.

At that moment, the possibility of realizing a common destiny among key nations and cultures of the world, centered on Europe, Russia, and China was coming into existence. This is the concept later developed by Gottfried Leibniz—and advocated today by Lyndon and Helga LaRouche, as embodied in the One Belt, One Road conception.

The reunification achieved at the Council of Florence, however, was short-lived. After the death of Zheng He, during his last voyage in 1433, the Chinese discontinued their ambitious navigational project. In 1453, with the help of the Venetians, the Ottoman Turks took over Constantinople.

Nicolaus of Cusa responded with his dialogue *On the Peace of Faith,* in

Zheng He statue in the Quanzhou Maritime Museum.

which he argued for unity in diversity among all humanity, based on the fact that all human beings are created in the living image of the Creator,—what the Chinese today call a *win-win approach.* The characters in the dialogue include representatives of European, Indian, Arab, Persian, Tatar, and other cultures. As Toscanelli's letter to Ferdinand Martin indicates, the ruler of Cathay or China at the time of Marco Polo was the Great Khan, who was a Tatar.

Before Cusanus' death, he convened a synod to reform the Catholic Church, from his position as Vicar General of the Papal States. Unfortunately, Cusanus' reform effort failed at that time because of the oligarchical corruption in Europe, reflected in the Curia.

Cusanus died in 1464: It was left to his immediate associates Toscanelli and Ferdinand Martin to continue his vision and to outflank the Venetian corruption then dominating Europe.

In 1476 Christopher Columbus was shipwrecked in

Zheng He's fleet, 1405, artist's rendition.

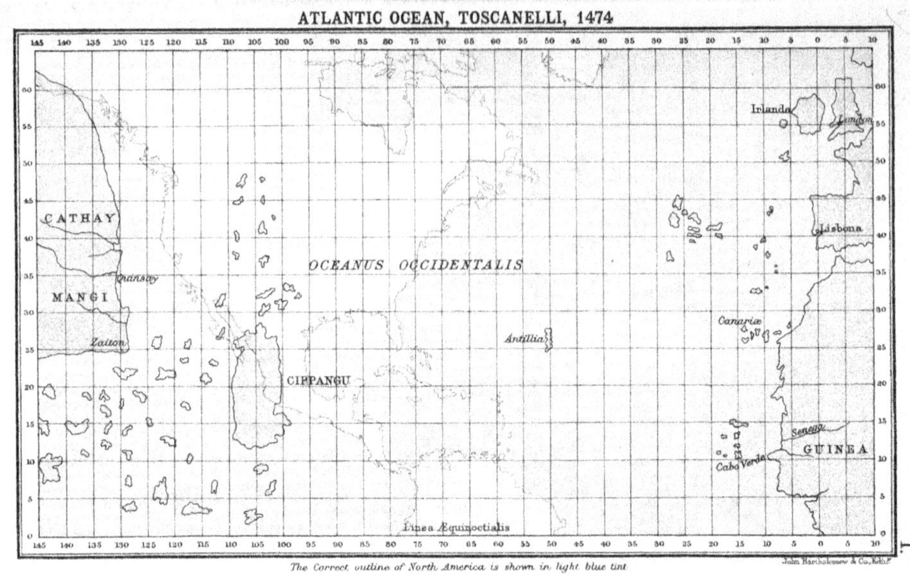

Toscanelli's map of 1474, with actual outline of North America shown in light blue.

Portugal, where he was befriended by Ferdinand Martin. Guided by his correspondence with Martin's collaborator Toscanelli, Christopher Columbus became the indispensable instrument for furthering the grand design, which, through the rediscovery of the Western Hemisphere and the creation of the United States of America, is now once again on the agenda. This time we must win!

Toscanelli's Letter to Ferdinand Martin (1474)

To Fernan Martinez, Canon of Lisbon,
Paulus the Physician sends greetings.

It pleased me to hear of your intimacy and friendship with your great and powerful King [Afonso V]. Often before have I spoken of a sea route from here to India, the land of spices; a route that is shorter than that via Guinea. You tell me that His Highness wishes me to explain this in greater detail so that it will be easier to understand, and to take this route. Although I could show this on a globe representing the earth, I have decided to do it more simply and clearly by demonstrating the way on a nautical chart. I therefore send His Majesty a chart drawn by my own hand, on which I have indicated the western coastline from Ireland in the north to the end of Guinea, and the islands that lie along this path. Opposite them, directly to the west, I have indicated the beginning of India, together with the islands and places you will come to; how far you should keep from the Arctic Pole and the Equator; and how many leagues you must cover before you come to these places, which are most rich in all kinds of spices, gems, and precious stones. Do not be amazed when I say that spices grow in lands to the west, even though we usually say the east; for he who sails west will always find these lands in the west, and he who travels east by land will always find the same lands in the east.

The upright lines on this chart show the distance from east to west, whereas the cross lines show the distance from north to south. The chart also indicates various places in India that may be reached if one meets with a storm or head-wind, or any other misfortune.

That you may know as much about these places as possible, you should know that the only people living on any of these islands are merchants who trade there.

There are said to be as many ships, mariners, and goods there as in the rest of the world put together. Especially in the principal port called Zaiton [Marco Polo's Zaitum, probably Quanzhou], where they load and unload a hundred great ships of pepper every year, not to mention many other ships with other spices. That country has many inhabitants, provinces, kingdoms, and innumerable cities, all of which are ruled by a prince known as the Great Khan—which in our language means 'The King of Kings'—who mainly resides in the province of Cathay.

His forefathers greatly desired to make contact with the Christian world, and some two hundred years ago they sent ambassadors to our Pope, asking him to send them many learned men who could instruct them in our faith. But these ambassadors met with difficulties on the way and had to turn back without reaching Rome. In the days of Pope Eugenius, there came an ambassador to him, who told him of their great feelings of friendship for the Christians. I had a long conversation with the ambassador about many things: about the vast size of the royal buildings, about the amazing length and breadth of their rivers, and about the great number of cities on their banks—so great a number that along one river there were two hundred cities with very long, wide bridges of marble that were adorned with many pillars.

This country is richer than any other yet discovered, and not only could it provide great profit and many valuable things, but also possesses gold and silver and precious stones and all kinds of spices in large quantities—things that do not reach our countries at present. There are also many scholars, philosophers, astronomers, and other men skilled in the natural sciences who govern that great kingdom and conduct its wars.

From the city of Lisbon to the west, the chart shows twenty-six sections, of two hundred and fifty miles each—altogether, nearly one-third of the earth's circumference before reaching the very large and magnificent city of Quinsay. This city is approximately one hundred miles in circumference, possesses ten marble bridges, and its name means 'The Heavenly City' in our language. Amazing things have been related about its vast buildings, its artistic treasures, and its revenues. It lies in the province of Manji, near the province of Cathay, where the king chiefly resides. And from the island of Antillia, which you call the Island of the Seven Cities, to the very famous island of Cipangu are ten sections, that is 2,500 miles. That island is very rich in gold, pearls, and precious stones, and its temples and palaces are covered in gold. But since the route to this place is not yet known, all these things remain hidden and secret; and yet one may go there in great safety.

I could still tell of many other things, but as I have already told you of them in person, and as you are a man of good judgment, I will write no further on the subject. I have tried to answer your questions as well as the lack of time and my work have permitted me, but I am always prepared to serve His Highness and answer his questions at greater length should he so wish.

Paolo dal Pozzo Toscanelli (1397-1482)

Written in Florence on the 25th of June. 1474.[3]

Toscanelli's Letter to Columbus (1480)

Paul, the physician to Christopher Columbus, greeting. I received your letters with the things you sent me, and with them received great satisfaction. I perceive your magnificent and grand desire to navigate from parts of the East to the West in the way that was set forth in the letter that I sent you and which will be demonstrated better on a round sphere. It pleases me much that I should be well understood: for the voyage is not only possible, it is true, and certain to be honorable and to yield incalculable profit, and a very great fame among all Christians. But you cannot know this perfectly save through experience and practice as I have had in the form of the most copious and good and true information from distinguished men of great learning who have come here in the [Papal] court of Rome [Florence at that time] from the said parts and from others being merchants, who have had business for a long time in those parts, men of high authority. Thus when that voyage shall be made it will be to powerful kingdoms and cities and most noble provinces, very rich in all manner of things in great abundance and very necessary to us, such as all sorts of spices in great quantity and jewels in greatest abundance.[4]

---

3. The source of this letter is *The Journals of Christopher Columbus*: In footnote 2, p. 4, it reads: "A copy of the original letter from Toscanelli to Martins in the handwriting of Columbus himself was found in the Columbine Library at Seville in 1860. It was a flyleaf of a book by Eneas Silvius, which formerly belonged to the Admiral. It is printed in Asensio's *Life of Columbus* (I, p. 250), and the above is translated from the text of Asensio. A Spanish version is given by Las Casas I, p. 92 and an Italian version in the *Vita del Ammiraglio*, cap. xiii." Eneas Silvius was Enea Silvio Bartolomeo Piccolomini (October 18, 1405 to August 14, 1464). He was Pope Pius II from August 19, 1458 to his death in 1464. In 1459, Pope Pius II appointed Nicolaus of Cusa the General Vicar of the Papal States.

4. http://www.latinamericanstudies.org/columbus/Columbus-Journal.pdf

Einstein Was Right: Only a Fool Keeps Repeating His Mistakes

by Helga Zepp-LaRouche

Sept. 30—That German Chancellor Angela Merkel, in spite of crushing losses for the parties of her Grand Coalition, said, "I don't see what else we should have done," points to a very common problem in the trans-Atlantic, neo-liberal Establishment, including Hillary Clinton. And maybe Mrs. Merkel even believes it: When someone is so totally convinced of the legitimacy of his or her remaining in power as an end in itself, it never occurs to that person that there is a deeper lawfulness which, when violated, takes revenge, and that there are completely different options for how history could develop.

This Establishment operates on the principle of "more of the same." In that regard, Einstein commented that to keep doing the same thing and expect different results is the very definition of insanity. But, given the acute danger of a new financial crisis, much worse than that of 2007-2008, that is extremely worrying.

If former CSU head Franz Josef Strauss could see the maneuvers of his party today, he would feel totally vindicated in his exasperated statement that the comparative of "enemy" is "deadly enemy," and the superlative is "fellow party member."

As for the SPD? Is it willing to reflect on why it was got the worst results since the Bismarck era, while Jeremy Corbyn and the Labour Party in Great Britain had the largest increase in votes since 1945? Obviously not. That is shown by the fact that the SPD describes Andrea Nahles, who as Labor Minister toughened the Hartz4 labor law, as the "left-wing of the party," and plans to appoint her head of the SPD parliamentary group. [Hartz4 forces the unemployed to take jobs at as little as $1.18 a day.]

courtesy of James Rea

Chancellor Angel Merkel Sept. 25, the day after her CDU Party's drubbing in the German elections.

Those who present themselves as the "saviors of the EU" are just as detached from reality, be they EU Commission head Jean-Claude Juncker, EU Council president Donald Tusk, or French President Emmanuel Macron—whose timing for his speech on the future of the EU on Sept. 26 proved to be worse than unfortunate, in light of the election results in Germany. [Among the measures Macron proposed were an EU Finance Minister and an EU budget.]

Given the Alternative for Germany's (*AfD*) election results, it can hardly be expected that the conservative wings of the CDU/CSU and the FDP will be persuaded to accept such new EU designs, which would give the *AfD* more momentum, and threaten to cost the German taxpayers even more. The attempt to perpetuate a system that seeks to defend the privileges of the few at the expense of those who have little with which to defend themselves, can and will not work.

Now there is an attempt to form a "Jamaica coalition" among the CDU/CSU, FDP, and Greens, whose party colors (black, yellow, green) correspond to those of the Jamaican flag. But given the fundamental political differences among the three parties—concerning a cap on refugees, financial policy, relations with Russia—it could take months before such a coalition could be formed, or even a new Grand Coalition, perhaps without Angela Merkel this time. But long before that could happen, a new financial crisis could break out, which would suddenly put the "state of emergency" which SPD politician Thomas Oppermann recently said has not "yet" arrived, on the agenda.

SPD politician Thomas Oppermann.

cc/Olaf Kosinsky

A Crisis Worse than 2007-8

Shortly before the Federal elections, Deutsche Bank published a report with the title "The Next Financial Crisis," which included a clear warning: "We are rather certain that there will soon be either a new financial crisis or a financial shock." Similar warnings are piling up—from *Spiegel* and *Die Welt*, the former Italian Economics and Financial Minister Giulio Tremonti, the Adam Smith Institute, and even 15 German and French economists, among them Clemens Fuest of the Institute for Economic Research (IFO) and Marcel Fratscher of the Berlin Economic Research Institute (DIW). They are all speaking of the immediate danger of a repeat of the crisis of 2008.

In reality, the entire trans-Atlantic financial system is like a minefield, where there are dozens of potential detonators. One of them is the indebtedness of American corporations. Thanks to the zero interest rate policy of 2010 to 2016, American corporations' indebtedness has risen from 7 to 14 trillion dollars, and in the current year alone, by 800 billion. These debts have already been bundled by Wall Street banks again into the notorious collateralized loan obligations (CLOs), with whose help these already worthless junk bonds will be resold.

Bloomberg wrote on September 26 that nothing is stopping these corporations from issuing these junk bonds simultaneously to two, three, or more investors, thus putting themselves in a position where they cannbot pay. If these companies then go bankrupt, the losses are by no means factored in, as the analysts like to describe it, euphemistically. When the toy company Toys 'R Us recently went bankrupt, the market price of its approximately 5 billion shares collapsed to only 20 cents on the dollar, not the 40 cents on the dollar which the investors had anticipated.

World Economic Forum/Greg Beadle

Chancellor Merkel's Former Federal Minister of Finance, enforcer of the EU's deadly banking policies that have devastated southern European countries.

But the Italian banking crisis (which the ECB, in panic over the threat of systemic collapse, allowed to be dealt with once again by forgetting the oft-cited "rules"); the impact of a possible secession of Catalonia from Spain on the Eurozone; the unmarketable "level three derivatives," as well as the total indebtedness of states, car dealers, U.S. students, or a huge "credit incident"—these are all only different aspects of the same problem. That is that this casino economy based on maximizing profits, which nearly hurled the world into chaos in 2007-8, today stands on the edge of a new, even more dangerous collapse, because all the "instruments" of the central banks—such as money printing and even negative interest rates—have been exhausted.

Perhaps the resignation of Wolfgang Schäuble as Finance Minister has something to do with the fact that he understands the complete mess which he is leaving behind.

One may assume that the various "saviors of Europe," who are demanding a European finance minister and a European budget—as well as the economists who are calling for an urgent reform of the EU—also understand the state of the financial system. That is why they have very concrete proposals as to how the burden is to be passed, through a combination of bailouts (to the taxpayer), bail-ins (to bank customers), and transfer payments (to German savers). The results of any such a scenario would be absolute chaos.

Glass-Steagall Is Urgent

There is only one other realistic alternative. Since President Trump has begun to circumvent his neo-con opposition in the Republican Party by working with Congressional Democrats to tackle overall budget questions, such as emergency assistance for the states destroyed by hurricanes, chances have grown that he will make good on one of his election promises: the reinstatement of Glass-Steagall banking separation. The Sept. 26 webinar, organized by Public Citizen and the Democratic Party group spun out of Bernie Sanders' campaign (Our Revolution), hosted by the AFL-CIO, and featuring remarks by Congressional representatives Marcy Kaptur and Walter Jones, was very encouraging in this respect.

The immediate introduction of Glass-Steagall—that is, the separation of commercial and investment banking, the writing-off of unpayable outstanding contracts,

as well as the eventual creation of a credit system based on financing the physical economy, rather like the tradition of the German Reconstruction Finance Corporation (*Kredit Anstalt für Wiederaufbau*) after the Second World War—is the only chance to avoid a disaster.

Chinese President Xi Jinping has often offered all nations cooperation with the new, rapidly developing economic and financial model of the New Silk Road. Instead of trying in the old geopolitical manner to contain China and its Belt and Road Initiative—an effort that won't succeed anyway—Germany and the other European nations should participate in the many building projects underway: the construction of infrastructure in East and Central Europe and the Balkans, and the construction of Silk Road hubs in Greece, Italy, Spain, and Portugal. The economic reconstruction of Syria, Iraq, Afghanistan, and above all, the entire African continent offers a fantastic perspective—for German small and medium-sized industry, and for the productive full-employment of currently jobless youth all over Europe.

The necessity for reorganizing a bankrupt financial system—the system which is responsible for opening the unbearable chasm between rich and poor, and whose injustice has prepared the ground for Brexit, the defeat of Hillary Clinton, the "no" in the Italian referendum, and now the miserable election results of the Grand Coalition—should not be so hard to recognize. The economic devastation of the new (eastern) Federal states, which the policy of the *Treuhand* under Birgit Breuel began, was the expression of an unjust system. Without this experience, the depopulation of whole villages, and the feeling of having been shoved to the very edge of society, despite the renewed town squares, the reaction in Eastern Germany to the refugee crisis would never have been so strong, and the *AfD* would not now be the strongest party in Saxony and the second strongest in the other four new federal states in the East.

Despite ongoing censorship by the mainstream media, a totally new economic system is growing, one which rests on totally different principles, namely on the common welfare of mankind and "win-win" cooperation among participating nations. It is in Germany's most essential interest to cooperate in this new paradigm.

Einstein was right: "One can never solve problems with the same kind of thinking that created them!"

II. And in America Today

China's Vision for a New Silk Road: A Nightmare for Evil People, But a Dream for Mankind

Sept. 30—Helga Zepp-LaRouche was interviewed by "V the Guerrilla Economist," a contributor to the Rogue Money website, on Sept. 28, 2017. An edited transcript follows.

V the Guerilla Economist: Today is Thursday, 10 AM on the Eastern seaboard of the United States and we have a very special guest—in fact we have two guests: We have none other than Harley Schlanger, who needs no introduction; and we have a very, very, very special guest, who I'm absolutely humbled to have on. We have Helga Zepp-La-Rouche, who is a German political activist. Many have called her the Mother of the Silk Road. She is the wife of none other than the famous Lyndon LaRouche. They are the creators and founders of La-Rouche PAC, as well as the Schiller Institute.

Incredible opportunity here, so without further ado, I'm going to hand it over to Harley. Harley, why don't you introduce Helga and give a little bit of a background, and then Helga, feel free to take this program however you want and for as long as you want. Go ahead.

Harley Schlanger: Thank you. Helga is probably most well-known for the founding of the Schiller Institute in 1984, and since that time, the Schiller Institute

has played an increasingly important role in shaping events in world history. And I think rather than saying anything more about it, we'll just let her tell you what she's up to and what her view is of the strategic situation. So, Helga, why don't you start and give us a sense of where you think things stand right now in the world?

Helga Zepp-LaRouche: What I would like to start with is something which I think is the most important, and which is, unfortunately, not well known in the United States and in Western Europe: It is a fact that there is, already, a completely new model of economics, of international relations among nations, and of a completely different paradigm. I think if people would know more about it, they would have much more hope for the future. What I'm talking about is that there is right now a New Silk Road dynamic. The old Silk Road, which connected cultures and nations about 2,000 years ago, and which exchanged not only goods but also especially technologies, cultures and ideas, laid the foundation for the economic wellbeing of all the participating nations. This was during the Han Dynasty.

In the recent period—exactly four years ago—President Xi Jinping revived that policy and he called it the New Silk Road. In these four years, this policy has taken off like a rocket. It is already now the largest in-

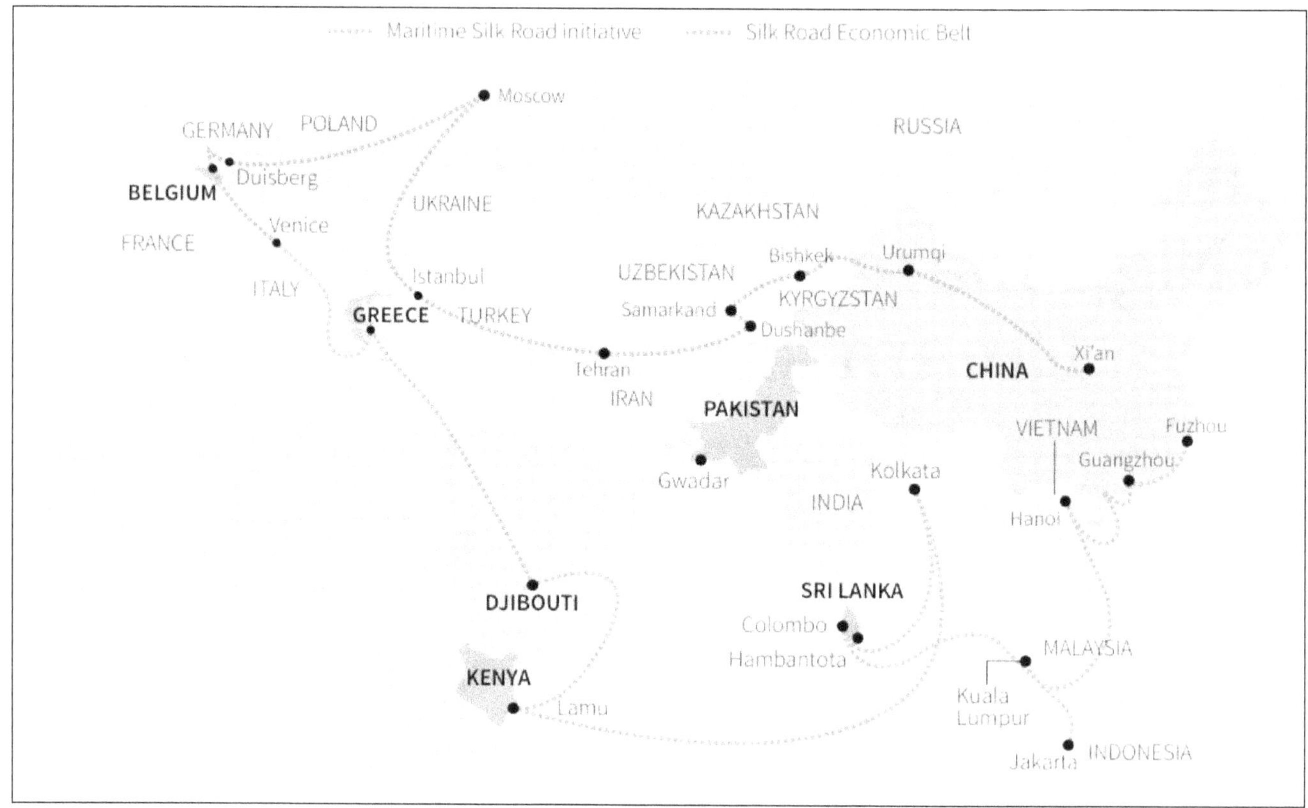

frastructure program in history. People are saying it's maybe twelve times or even twenty times as big as the Marshall Plan was in the postwar period for the reconstruction of Europe. And, it involves the collaboration of more than seventy countries. To put it in a nutshell, China—which I had the fortune to visit already in 1971 in the middle of the Cultural Revolution—especially in the last thirty years, has made gigantic progress in economic development. They have lifted 700 million people out of poverty, and the Chinese economic miracle is the most impressive economic miracle in history, ever, even bigger than the German economic miracle in the postwar period. China is now simply offering that model to all participating countries, providing an infrastructure connection among the different countries, and it is just taking off.

I think if Americans who are right now in a real hardship—with all these hurricanes in Texas and then Florida and Puerto Rico—only knew about the potential of that program, they would have a completely different outlook for the future. So I would like to talk more about it, if you want me to.

V: Yes, please.

Zepp-LaRouche: First of all, the New Silk Road is based on "win-win cooperation." Most people in the West cannot imagine that any government would be devoted to the common good and also have an interest in the common good of the other nation, because in the last fifty years or so—I would say since the assassination of John F. Kennedy—foreign policy was always based on geopolitics: you have to defend your interests against another nation. And in the Bush and Obama period you had interventionist wars to change regimes. Because of these policies, people have the wrong idea of what policy can be.

But I'm telling you as a person who has been involved with China for more than forty years, that I really have come to the conclusion that China has offered a new model of win-win cooperation: China is pursuing its own interests, but it is also at the same time, making sure that the other country is fulfilling its own interests. And that is simply a completely different model of cooperation: They have the win-win cooperation policy for infrastructure development with a completely new financial system which goes along with that, which is the Asian Infrastructure Investment Bank, the AIIB; the New Silk Road Fund, and the New Development Bank which goes along with the BRICS countries which are cooperating with this project. And these new financial institutions offer credit for infrastructure financing.

It's a completely different model. It's not like Wall Street or the City of London, looking toward high-profit revenues of 20-25%. Rather it starts from the understanding that without infrastructure there can be no economic development and no agricultural development. So in a certain sense, it's not profit oriented, but it's oriented to create the framework for industrial development.

So you have infrastructure development and a new financial system, but you also have a new model of foreign policy, based on the absolute respect for the sovereignty of the other country, based on the respect for the different social system of the other nation. In that sense, it may sound funny to American ears, but when President Trump talked about the American System, and the Chinese model, they have much more in common than you would ever think if you just read the *New York Times*.

I think it is really an incredible new model, and I wish to encourage people to find out more about it. If you want to learn more about it, you can visit many Chinese websites, but you also can go to our website of the Schiller Institute and the Schiller Institute's New Paradigm page where we have featured many, many projects and many conferences. Right now, President Trump is faced with the incredible task of the necessity of financing the reconstruction of these states which have been hit by these hurricanes. Given the combination of powers in the House and in the Senate, two days ago he had a meeting in the White House with Democrats and rejected the public-private partnership—PPP—model as a way of financing the reconstruction.

Since 2015, we have promoted the idea that the best way for U.S. infrastructure to be built—even long before these hurricanes hit—would be for the United States join with the New Silk Road and take up the offer of President Xi Jinping to President Trump when they met for the first time in Mar-a-Lago in April, that the United States should cooperate with China on building the New Silk Road, even inside the United States.

V: Helga, let me ask you this question: Why do you think the Atlanticists, the British, and the deep state influence that's here in the United States—why do you think they are *so* resistant to the Silk Road? I know China's been calling on the United States from the beginning saying, "Hey, c'mon, get involved, there's a lot of money to be made here, everybody can prosper, everybody can be successful, and you'll be helping many nations," and time, and time, and time again, the politicians here in the United States have always said, "no." Why do you think that is, Helga?

Zepp-LaRouche: The concept of "oligarchy" is really important to be understood, because the trans-Atlantic establishment is really an oligarchy in the old tradition of empires: the idea that you have a small elite which has all the privileges, and they form a club, and they have rules and these rules must be followed by those people who want to be members of the club. And they do that to the detriment of most of the population.

For example, why did the German election just now go in the same direction—a rejection of that policy? Because the majority of the people are the victims of this globalization. So, these Atlanticists, or neo-cons, or neo-liberals, whatever you want to call them—see an emerging paradigm which is for the benefit of the common good; they can see that. The reason why the New Silk Road is so attractive is because people benefit from it! And this old oligarchy sees that this new model is much more attractive to the population, but all of the privileges of the oligarchy rest on high-profit, high-risk speculation,—all this virtual paper of derivatives—something which has no real value. The reason why this oligarchy wants to stick to this system is that all of their privileges are associated with the system.

So in a certain sense, it's really like an old oligarchy, with entrenched powers, and they don't want to give it up. But I think it's a question of time, because the new paradigm is already emerging, and since it is so much more attractive for the common people, I think it will win.

V: Yeah. Can you detail for us some of the latest developments with the New Silk Road and One Belt, One Road Initiative? I see there are some clues that are being given. For instance, we now have Saudi Arabia meeting with President Putin; China is launching their new gold settlement, petro-yuan standard, for purposed of pricing oil in the Asian markets, which I think eventually

Xinhua

Addis Ababa-Djibouti Railroad, Ethiopia.

wikipedia

Bui Dam and hydroelectic station, Ghana.

Xinhua

Africa Standard Gauge Railway, Kenya.

Xinhua

China-Europe train.

chinca.org

Coca Codo Sinclair Dam, Ecuador.

www.gwadarport.gov

Port of Gwadar, Pakistan.

will go worldwide as a replacement for the petrodollar.

What other major events are happening? Because I think the way the New Silk Road is being built up, it is unavoidable, and you simply cannot ignore it.

Zepp-LaRouche: There are many things, but the most dramatic is the Chinese investments in Africa. For many centuries, colonialism left Africa in a horrible condition. Subsequently, IMF conditionalities pre-

vented any real development. There was very clearly, from the side of the West, no intention to ever industrialize Africa. Look at the horrible conditions which caused the refugee crisis, thousands of people drowning in the Mediterranean, fleeing from hunger and war—there was no intention of the West to do anything efficient about that.

With the New Silk Road development, China has simply brought the new development approach to

Africa. They have built a railroad between Djibouti and Addis Ababa, 750 km, which is already functioning. They're in the process of building other railroads from Kenya all the way to Rwanda. They have also built many hydropower dams, industrial parks, and agricultural development projects. And most recently the Chinese government and the Italian government have agreed to do a feasibility study for what will become the largest infrastructure project in history, ever: the Transaqua project.

Transaqua is something we have been supporting for decades. The idea was more recently developed by Italian engineers, to bring some of the surplus water of the Congo River tributaries—these tributaries are at an altitude of 500 meters—and you can build a canal system which brings the water down to Lake Chad, which has dried out and shrunk to about 10% of its previous volume. That way you would develop an internal shipping system for twelve countries; you would develop hydropower, water for irrigation; it would completely change the character of Africa.

So this is now seriously on the agenda. I have talked recently to many Africans who are, for the first time, culturally optimistic, that they can overcome hunger and poverty in the short term—a perspective of hope which the African continent never had before! And that has changed their self-confidence, so African leaders no longer want to listen to the sermons and advice from the European Union, for example, about "good governance," when these Europeans never offered any development. They're now saying, we want to be treated as equal partners. We want to have direct investment: And China has offered to join hands with all countries, because obviously, if you want to industrialize the African continent the opportunities are enormous.

And there are some economists who agree with us, that while China is now an absolutely incredible economic miracle, Africa will be an even more gigantic development miracle following that.

So I think it has completely changed the world, and I'm very optimistic that this will become the way we will reshape all the relations among nations. And we will overcome geopolitics: This is the most important. If all the nations cooperate in a win-win policy, you do not need geopolitics any more. Geopolitics has caused two world wars in the last century, and obviously, with thermonuclear weapons, we cannot afford to have war as a means of conflict resolution. With the New Silk Road, that option is on the table, and as dangerous as

the North Korea situation is right now, I think but for the good relations between President Xi Jinping and President Trump, this conflict could have gotten out of control already; but fortunately, they telephone a lot, and so far they have been able to avoid complete disaster. Even so, it obviously remains extremely dangerous.

V: I agree with you. I think even in the North Korean situation there's a stability that can be brought there, because of the New Silk Road and some investment that China and Russia want to do in North Korea. Let's be honest: Last year, or the year before, it was discovered that North Korea has close to $10 trillion worth of rare earth deposits as well as strategic metals and minerals, and now, all of a sudden, the war rhetoric is starting to heat up amongst the Atlanticists. I don't think it's a coincidence to see all this saber rattling, so to speak, Helga. What say you?

Zepp-LaRouche: I think the geopolitical forces in the world consciously created this North Korea crisis to have an opportunity to work against Russia and China. Remember that an earlier South Korea President, Jim Dae-jung, already had a Sunshine Policy with North Korea: They were building an industrial zone in the north of South Korea, where the Russians, and North and South Korea worked together. That was then interrupted by Bush and Cheney, for no good reason. And the whole THAAD deployment and the military drills which the U.S.A. and South Korea are carrying out is a continuous provocation, in order to provide a pretext for a policy which is really an encirclement policy against Russia and China.

But this is being outflanked right now, because at the recent Eastern Economic Forum in Vladivostok, President Putin had a big meeting with the North Koreans and the South Koreans, and they discussed restarting the economic development zone in the northern part of South Korea, where Russia and the two Koreas would work together, with Chinese input, to put this back on the agenda.

As you said, the New Silk Road is really a prescription for peace, everywhere where you apply it! We have always said, if North Korean and South Korean engineers are working together on building railroads and industrialized areas, then the reason for war would be eliminated. And I think that that is the only path to solve that problem definitively.

Schlanger: I'd like to jump in here, and ask Helga to talk a little bit about the whole question of the New Silk Road and Europe, given the changes going on in Europe and the election in Germany: What's happening with the Italian banking system; Macron's proposal [in France]. Do you see a shift in Europe, an openness now toward the Chinese and the New Silk Road?

Zepp-LaRouche: It's unexpected, but I think it's coming here as well. First of all, the German situation after this election is total chaos! Merkel and the CDU/CSU, as well as the SPD both had their lowest election results ever. In the case of the SPD, the lowest since Bismarck, and in the case of the CDU, the lowest since the Second World War. They got payback for their neoliberal policies, which was the same reason Hillary Clinton lost the U.S. election. Merkel, like Hillary Clinton, is just not willing or capable of reflecting on the causes. So Merkel said she could not imagine having done anything better—and that's her problem: She can't think of anything better, and that's why she lost the election.

As a result, since the SPD said they would not go back to a grand coalition government, the only option left is a so-called "Jamaica coalition," which would be the CDU/CSU—and they have trouble now among themselves, so this is in a mess—and the liberals, the Free Democratic Party (FDP), and the Greenies. This is called "Jamaica" because these parties' colors are the same as the flag of Jamaica [black, gold, green]. But this may not function: You could have an unstable government for the rest of the year in Germany, because inside these parties you have tremendous frictions and faction fights.

I'm saying this because I think the danger of a new financial crash is high, and the signs for that are mounting. The EU used to be really run by the Merkel/Schäuble combination, but Schäuble will no longer be finance minister, because one of the preconditions for

Chinese-built high speed rail in Kenya.

Xinhua

the negotiations to form a new government, the FDP wants to have the Finance Ministry. So if a financial crash hits, at a time that we don't have a stable German government, you don't have a stable European Union either. If you look at all the other countries, the Southern European countries are completely unstable: Italy is a mess; in France, Macron won the election on the second round, but he fell in the polls and he's now regarded as a liberal, so you can forget his famous proposal for a new European Union. It's in the wastepaper basket, because he clearly conceptualized that speech for a different German election outcome than what actually happened.

What you have instead is that the attractiveness of the New Silk Road for East and Central European countries is enormous: The so-called 16+1 [16 Eastern and Central European countries plus China], they all want to cooperate with the New Silk Road. The Balkan countries want to cooperate; Greece, Serbia, Hungary and even Poland, they're all on the bandwagon. The same goes for Italy, which together with Greece, was worst-hit by the refugee crisis, and between the Italian and the Chinese government there are many discussions and agreements that they have to cooperate in developing Africa as the only way to overcome the refugee catastrophe.

Even Spain's Prime Minister Rajoy is now fully on-board. He wants Spain to be a hub for the New Silk Road, not only that it should be the Western end of the Eurasian New Silk Road, but he wants to have Spain to be the hub in the connection to Ibero-America. The same goes for Portugal, where they want to become the hub, not only for Ibero-America, but also for the Portuguese speaking countries in Africa.

Switzerland is entirely in favor of the New Silk Road. Austria is also absolutely for it.

I have said for a very long time that we have to surround Germany with Silk Road developments. The German government is still aligned with the European Union, which is hysterically against the New Silk Road. The EU tries to block some of the projects being built by China by saying that "we have to insist on the rules, we set the standards," but these countries don't want to listen to the European Union when they can have a high-speed rail line built built by—and connected to—China. The EU is clearly on the losing end in this.

Right now the spirit of the New Silk Road is slowly but steadily coming into Germany. You have literally dozens of conferences taking place on a local level in Munich, in Stuttgart, in Cologne, in Koblenz,—just all over—Chambers of Commerce, industrial associations, and they all have their Silk Road events, because they realize that for industry this is the future. So I don't think that this can be stopped. It's just a question of whether we can get results quick enough, before chaos strikes: If you have a new financial crash, without having some alternative in place, it could end up in chaos, and there, actually, is the biggest danger.

V: That's excellent to know. What other developments are there? We talked about Europe; we talked about Africa. Are there any inroads that China's making in the Western Hemisphere? What's in South America, maybe Canada, or anything like that?

Zepp-LaRouche: There are several countries in Ibero-America that are absolutely catching on: Peru,

video grab, www.news.cn

Matthew Pottinger, a member of the U.S. National Security Council of the administration of President Trump to oversee Asian affairs, represented Trump at the May 14-15 Belt and Road forum in Beijing.

Brazil, Bolivia, Chile, and Ecuador. Now the project for the Bioceanic Railway is seriously on the agenda, to be built from Brazil to Peru; and another rail line is to go through Bolivia. This is very important, because, like Africa, before this Chinese investment started, if you looked at the map of Latin America or Africa, there was absolutely no infrastructure connecting across the continent linking the coasts, or connecting to the interior of the continent. Now, with this Bioceanic Railway, you have for the very first time, something which was first considered by Alexander von Humboldt [in the 19th Century]. And naturally it was promoted by my husband, Lyndon LaRouche, when he worked with President José López Portillo of Mexico on "Operation Juárez," which was his proposal in 1982 to have an Ibero-American infrastructure integration. So now all these things we have been campaigning for are, step by step, coming true; so I feel vindicated, also for the life's work of my husband.

V: Absolutely. Harley, do you have any questions for Helga?

Schlanger: I would like to get Helga's thoughts on the Trump Administration, where we see the prospect of the Trump-Xi Jinping meeting in November: Things have to happen pretty quickly. What do you think, Helga? Any possibility that we can see some change? You mentioned earlier that Trump seemed to indicate in a meeting with Democrats that infrastructure has to be government funded, rather than private partnerships.

Zepp-LaRouche: Xi Jinping campaigned for Trump to attend the Belt and Road Forum in May in Beijing. This was a very big summit, with twenty-nine world leaders addressing it—Xi Jinping, Putin, and others, and we campaigned

An aerial view of the core zone of the Tianjin Binhai-Zhongguancun Science and Technology Park, to which hi-tech industries have relocated from Beijing.

strongly, calling on Trump to attend, that that should be the occasion for the United States and China to reach out and work together on this. Well, this did not quite succeed, but we may have had an influence that there was a very important representative sent—Matthew Pottinger, who attended the Belt and Road Forum. There have been many events since between Chinese and Americans in New York and elsewhere, and I think there actually is a steady process of integration and dialogue in four different categories. Economics, security, people-to-people exchanges—all of this is going on. If President Trump goes to China in November, as is now being prepared by Secretary of State Tillerson, and considering that Commerce Secretary Ross Wilbur was just in China, I think there is the potential to really upgrade, and I cannot imagine that Trump would go and not come back with really not just something on North Korea and trade, but a vision.

I think President Trump has surprised both his supporters and his opponents again and again, that despite all of these attacks on him, he has not given up, and he has come out again and again with principled policies. So, I think the fact that in the past he had mentioned the American System, the policies of Alexander Hamilton, Henry Carey, Lincoln, Glass-Steagall—all of these things are still on the agenda. Now, he should join hands with the New Silk Road development. I have written an article, which was distributed at the Belt and Road

Forum, where I basically said, the Chinese have $1.4 trillion in foreign reserves in U.S. Treasuries. If they just sit on this paper, it doesn't mean anything for them, but if they would invest this money through an infrastructure bank, or better through a National Bank, in infrastructure in the United States, such Chinese investment could go a very long way to help finance rebuilding U.S. infrastructure, and thus kick-start such a program. Chinese firms—China Invest Corp. for example—have said that the infrastructure requirement of the United States is not $1 trillion as Trump has said, but actually $8 trillion!

I have the idea that the United States should do what China is doing in terms of high-speed rail. China has built already, as of the end of last year, more than 20,000 km of high-speed rail; they're now building high-speed trains which will top 400 kmh, and cruise at about 330 mph. These high-speed rail systems in China are *really good*. They're smooth, quiet, and they're planning now to connect every major city in China by 2020—that's an enormous perspective. I think the United States urgently needs a fast train system: The infrastructure in the United States really needs modernization, and why not go, really, for a big program right from the beginning, to connect all the big cities through high-speed rail, while building a couple of new cities! You have the East and the West Coast which are pretty developed, but all the states in between, they

Chaobaihe Bridge, which will connect Beijing's Tongzhou District and Hebei's Yanjiao County, under construction on November 27, 2016.

could easily take a couple of new modern cities—science cities, research cities—and I think it would inject into the American population a sense of great optimism, providing a vision of the future, which is very difficult right now because of the heritage of the last two administrations.

So I think this visit could really become a breakthrough, and obviously, our organization—LaRouche PAC in the United States—we are fully mobilizing to get precisely that on the agenda. And I would like our listeners to really help. If you want to do something good for the United States, note that Trump said again, recently, that he likes the Chinese, that he likes Xi Jinping, and that is clearly something people should start thinking about: Why is Trump saying that? And I fully agree, the Chinese model right now is something to study, and the world can only profit if the two nations, the United States and China, find a way to cooperate on this development. I think this will be absolutely decisive for history at this moment.

V: Absolutely, I agree with that. For world powers like the United States and China, and even Russia, to cooperate, and communicate and to help build a better world, is something so remarkable, and I think it will usher in a new era of peace such as the world has never seen, and I guess that is a nightmare to some of these cabal Atlanticists, some of these individuals you see up in the halls of power, and in the City of London and Wall Street, as well as Washington, D.C.

Zepp-LaRouche: Yes! I think it's a nightmare for the evil people, but it's a dream for mankind.

Schlanger: V, one of the things I'd like to propose, is that since Helga's going to begin doing a weekly briefing in the United States, we can get a link to you at *Rogue Money* that you could put up, so people can get regular updates from her.

V: Absolutely. Absolutely. We could definitely do that, and we'll definitely get that done. We'll get that set up, and when you have that link, we'll go right to *Rogue Money* and blast that through all our networks, and put it out to all our distribution as well. Thanks for allowing us to do that.

Helga, your closing comments and anything else you want to say? And how can people follow you in your work?

Zepp-LaRouche: People should just have the idea that we are at a turning point in history. Most people don't think in terms of the long arcs of history; they think about events and news and breaking developments, but I, because of my relationship and marriage with my husband, I have started to think in terms of long arcs of history. And you can actually see that we are right now at a turning point: I always say, the way to imagine the new paradigm that is emerging, is that it is as different from what has existed up to now, as the Middle Ages were with respect to the modern era. What separated these two was the Italian Renaissance, and with that emerged the completely different idea of the individual, of science, of the state. You know, in the Middle Ages, people believed in superstitions, you had the scholastics, the Aristotelians, and they had a different set of axioms of belief than what came with the Italian Renaissance: Namely the idea that man is endlessly perfectible, that the state needs to be devoted to the common good, and there were many ideas, which would take too long to go into; but it led to completely different axioms of thinking, and everything we enjoy today, in terms of science, technology, culture, came really from that shift, especially Classical music, Classical poetry, all of these things.

That's the kind of change we are experiencing right now: What we used to associate with globalization, with Wall Street, with profit for a few and poverty for many—all of this will go, and we enter a new paradigm where, as President Xi Jinping always says, "we are entering a community for a shared future of mankind," where the idea that we are one humanity, that that idea comes first, and that we will define the future, how we want to be in 100 years from now, or even 1,000 years from now. Do we still want to have wars, do we still want to kill each other? Obviously, not. We want to concentrate on the common aims of mankind, on thermonuclear fusion—research and commercial applications. If we reach that, we will have energy security; we will have raw materials security; we will have space transportation. We are only scratching the surface of what space is like. As a result of the recent findings of the Hubble Telescope, it is now known that we have two trillion galaxies—now that blows my mind. I cannot imagine two trillion galaxies, but that is out there! And we know absolutely only a tiny detail about it.

I think if we concentrate on the joint tasks of the future, people will start to grow up. For me, it's mankind growing up and that is very exciting. So I want people to be optimistic and be part of our movement. We are shaping the future in the best possible way by thinking this way.

V: Right, absolutely. With that being said, Helga LaRouche, thank you so much for being on, and Harley, thank you so much for being on as well, and thank you for setting up this interview. I want to thank the both of you, and we're looking forward to having Helga's weekly address in the United States broadcast through our channels as well.

Zepp-LaRouche: Thank you.

The New Silk Road Becomes the World Land-Bridge

The BRICS countries have a strategy to prevent war and economic catastrophe. It's time for the rest of the world to join!

This 374-page report is a road-map to the New World Economic Order that Lyndon and Helga LaRouche have championed for over 20 years.

Includes:

Introduction by Helga Zepp-LaRouche, "The New Silk Road Leads to the Future of Mankind!"

The metrics of progress, with emphasis on the scientific principles required for survival of mankind: nuclear power and desalination; the fusion power economy; solving the water crisis.

The three keystone nations: China, the core nation of the New Silk Road; Russia's mission in North Central Eurasia and the Arctic; India prepares to take on its legacy of leadership.

Other regions: The potential contributions of Southwest, Central, and Southeast Asia, Australia, Europe, and Africa.

The report is available in PDF $35 and in hard copy $50 (softcover) $75 (hardcover)
plus shipping and handling.

Order from http://store.larouchepub.com

Americans Must Understand What China Is Really Doing

The following remarks by Helga Zepp-LaRouche, and the ensuing dialogue, are from the LaRouche PAC Manhattan Meeting on Saturday, Sept. 30, 2017.

Helga Zepp-LaRouche: I am very happy to be able to speak to you. I would like to start with the grave crisis the United States is in because of these hurricanes. On the one side, naturally, it is absolutely terrible for the people who have suffered losses—lives have been lost, property has been lost, lives have been destabilized. But a great crisis can be turned into a great opportunity. The reason why I am saying that is you have President Trump, who said some extraordinary things with respect to Puerto Rico. He said that this has never been seen before—such a degree of devastation—but that this will also be the greatest recovery ever.

The only problem that has to be dealt with is what to do about the debt of Puerto Rico, but he earlier said that public-private partnerships (PPPs) don't function. So therefore, you have now a situation where not only Texas, Florida, and some of the other southern states have been devastated, but what the hurricane did to Puerto Rico is absolutely devastating.

The entirety of what little infrastructure existed there has been wiped out, and despite massive military efforts right now to rebuild, something very fundamental has to be done. This is right now a situation in which—as we have been saying all along— given the abysmal condition of the infrastructure in the United States, including the situation in New York, the terrible condition of the roads, the absence of a fast train system—you now have a terrible economic collapse, including a collapsing life expectancy. If you ever want to have a parameter for a collapsing society, then it is surely that.

We have said the whole time that given the fact that Congress is what it is—the neo-cons in the Republican Party are what they are—that only a bipartisan coalition implementing the Four Laws of Mr. LaRouche—Glass-Steagall, a national bank, a credit system—would provide the kind of financing necessary for the reconstruction not only of Puerto Rico, but of the entire United States. We have also said all along that, given the strategic environment, the only thing that makes sense is for the United States to take up the offer of President Xi Jinping and join with the New Silk Road. And that the United States should allow Chinese investments in U.S. infrastructure, allowing the Chinese to invest their ap-

President Donald Trump and President Xi Jinping at the G20 Summit in Hamburg, Germany, July 9, 2017.

proximately $1.4 trillion in U.S. Treasury bonds in American infrastructure. That is the case.

Such action is more urgent than ever, because all the signs are mounting that we are faced with a new financial crisis much worse than that of 2008. All of the parameters that warned us in 2007-2008 are warning us again, but they show conditions that are much worse, because the central banks in these almost ten years did absolutely nothing to remove the causes of the crash. Therefore you have now an absolutely hopeless financial situation in which, almost daily now, someone here or there is warning of the danger of a crash. So it is absolutely urgent.

wikipedia/Gage Skidmore
Steve Bannon

CC/Andrew Dallos
Hillary Clinton

Bannon and Hillary Are Wrong

Today is the last day of September; that means we have about six weeks until President Trump goes on a tour of Asia, where he will visit several countries. Secretary of State Tillerson is presently in Beijing preparing for Trump's tour. As it looks now, Trump will have a big state visit to China in November in the context of this Asia trip. If you go back to April, when President Trump was meeting with President Xi Jinping in Mar-a-Lago, in a quite significant reversal from what Trump had said during the election campaign, he did not continue China-bashing. Instead he found something which he has repeatedly called a friendship with President Xi. He has said repeatedly that he likes the Chinese, that they are a great people. And indeed, what has developed since Mar-a-Lago is a very important strategic partnership and relationship between President Trump and President Xi.

In April, we started a mobilization, demanding that President Trump attend the Belt and Road Forum in May. Well, this fell short of its objective a little bit, but we succeeded in creating an environment in which Trump sent a very important envoy, Matt Pottinger, to the Belt and Road Forum. Out of this whole process developed four strategic dialogues, which are functioning and which have resulted in prospects for potentially resolving major hotspots such as in North Korea.

As a matter of fact, just now, Secretary of State Tillerson said in Beijing that there are two or three back channels to North Korea. At the same time, a North Korean delegation was in Moscow, and Moscow signaled its readiness to work toward a political and diplomatic solution, which obviously would involve Russia, China, and the United States. So, this thing is working, and I would suggest that we go on an equal or even bigger mobilization than we did in April when we tried to get President Trump to the Beijing Belt and Road Forum.

We should somehow use this crisis in the United States to get across the concept that what is needed right now is the immediate implementation of Glass-Steagall and the Four Laws of Mr. LaRouche—but in combination with the concept of this strategic alliance between the United States and China, whereby the United States becomes part of the World Land-Bridge.

Now, there are some problems. One is Mr. Steve Bannon, who may have some merits, but his policy toward China is wrong. He just practically declared war on China, saying China is the biggest problem, the biggest threat. They are stealing American technology, he says, just to incorporate it and become a competitor. I don't know if he's just badly informed, or if he is ideologically so much in the geopolitical game that he can't see what is actually going on; I can't say for sure.

But obviously, the Obama-Hillary faction of the establishment, along with the neo-cons in the Republican Party, are all against an alliance of the United States with Russia and China, because that would end their geopolitical game and their aim to get a unipolar world, which they have been very explicit on trying to achieve. Now you have, in addition to that, the Bannon factor trying to work on Trump to try to pit him against China.

I think this is strategic, and we absolutely have to counter it, because the perception in the West of what China is actually doing is absolutely wrong.

A New Form of Relations Among States

Let me again throw in my authority, so to speak. I am not claiming to be an expert on China, but I can say that a lot of my life story has been interwoven with being—not involved,—but being privileged to see the gigantic rise of China. I was in China for the first time in 1971, during the Cultural Revolution, and I have visited many times since 1996, when we had already worked out the proposal for a Eurasian Land-Bridge, a New Silk Road idea. So I can say that what has happened in China—and people in the United States must really know about this—is the biggest economic miracle in history—a bigger economic miracle than that of the postwar reconstruction of Germany. China has now begun to export its own, gigantic economic miracle of the last thirty years.

China now has a very large middle section of the society—good income, good living standard; it has lifted more than 700 million people out of poverty. President Xi has just said that the Chinese government is going to use the Internet to help to lift the remaining 40 million or so people still in poverty in rural areas, by organizing e-commerce for people in these rural areas to be able to sell their produce, their agricultural products. This is typical of the Chinese, that they would come up with something like that. The idea is to eliminate poverty in China by the year 2020.

Now China has developed a new model of foreign policy, and it is really important that Americans familiarize themselves with that, because it is not that China is taking over like Bannon is saying—that China is somehow threatening to take the position of the United States. Some of you may remember that a couple of months ago, at a meeting in New York at which the Chinese Ambassador in Washington, Cui Tiankai, gave a presentation, he said that there were sixteen examples in history in which a country surpassed the then dominant power: that in twelve cases it led to war, and in four cases, the rising power just replaced the old dominant power.

Ambassador Cui said that China wants neither a future like one of the twelve cases in which war ensued, nor a future like that of the other four cases, because what China is offering is a completely new model of relations among states.

I want to go through this because I think it is absolutely key. China is proposing a new model for major powers, based on absolute respect for the sovereignty of the other states—including the principle of non-interference, the principle of the acceptance of another social model, and a win-win cooperation between the two of them. Now that is obviously what the relationship between the United States and China should become. An aspect of this new Chinese model is a new relationship with the neighbors of China. This is already in effect with the ASEAN countries, with the Shanghai Cooperation Organization; it's operational in the South China Sea, where countries that are neighbors recognize the benefits of mutual economic cooperation rather than geopolitical confrontation.

The third aspect, which is in one sense the most important, is that China has developed a completely new model for relationships with the developing countries. This is most visible on the African continent. The Belt and Road Initiative, the New Silk Road, is open-ended; that's the good thing. It has completely changed the character of the African continent, because the Chinese have built a railroad from Djibouti to Addis Ababa; they are now building railroads from Kenya and Mozambique all the way to Rwanda. They have built many industrial parks, hydroelectric power plants, and irrigation systems. Now they are planning to have the largest infrastructure program ever—the Transaqua program—which will transform the entire continent of Africa for sure.

This is a new model of relations, and it is not based on geopolitics. It has embodies the idea of an alliance of perfectly sovereign nation-states; it is actually what John Quincy Adams had proposed when he was Presi-

John Quincy Adams

dent of the United States—that the United States should work toward an alliance of such sovereign states. This is very important. One expression of the spirit of common development for the common good, is to have an international banking system devoted to investments in the real economy. Banks like the Asian Infrastructure Investment Bank (AIIB), the New Development Bank of the BRICS, the Maritime Silk Road Fund, the Silk Road Fund, and similar institutions—together, these are already a parallel financial system.

So if the United States were to end the casino economy (as we call it), go for Glass-Steagall, write off the non-payable outstanding contracts, write off the casino part of the economy, and go to a Hamiltonian system of banking—that would perfectly fit in with the already existing New Paradigm of the New Silk Road. This is not just an option; I think it is the only way we can get out of this mess.

Revolt of the Deliberately Forgotten

Then look at the rest of the so-called Western alliance. We have just had an election in Germany that has completely shattered the existing political configuration. Earlier, in the Brexit, the British people voted against the EU, against a neo-liberal economic system that makes the rich richer while the poor become poorer—the gap between rich and poor widens.

That spirit continued with the election of President Trump, or rather, the defeat of Hillary Clinton. It continued with the "No" vote in the Italian referendum last December, a vote against a measure that aimed to change the constitution to make it more suitable for the banking system, and this was rejected by the Italian people.

Then there is the German election. If you thought Germany was a stable country, well that is down the river. The SPD, the Social Democracy, had the worst result since Bismarck. Merkel's CDU lost and are now at a miserable level, a little bit more than 30 percent. And Merkel really only received about 29 percent, if you count all the votes.

This has led to a situation in which the SPD has rejected a continuation of the grand coalition, and the other parties are now trying to put together an alliance among the CDU/CSU, the FDP, and the Greens. But that is a very rocky road, because there are many opposing views on Russia, on the migrants, on the refugee crisis, on the power of the European Central Bank. So this may not lead to any big result in the near future, and the effort may even go into the beginning of next year; nobody knows if they will be able to form a government.

The most shocking aspect of the election results is that the right-wing populist party, the Alternative for Germany (AfD), received 12.5 percent and is now the third-largest force in Germany. In Saxony in East Germany, it became number one; it is now the strongest party in Saxony. In all the other new states formed from the so-called German "Democratic" Republic, the eastern states, they became the second-largest party. In that party—I'm not saying that all the people who voted for it are racists or Nazis—but you have some really evil Nazi types in leading positions. Two-thirds of those who voted for the AfD did so, not because they like the AfD, but because they wanted to teach the other parties a lesson. Nevertheless, if you look at the fact that in the east of Germany, the AfD is now number one and number two—well, what does that mean?

It means that the entire post fall-of-the-Wall political structure of Germany has just disintegrated. There is a great divide between East and West. In the West they want to form a so-called Jamaica coalition, which would include the CDU, CSU, FDP, and Greens, but these parties are not represented in the East. That is a big shock. Why did the AfD get so many votes in the East? I really think it is important to understand that it is essentially the same phenomenon that led to the defeat of Hillary Clinton.

In the Interest of the Other

What is the problem of this collapsing paradigm? When the Soviet Union collapsed, the neo-cons in the United States, together with the British, decided to impose shock therapy. They decided to smash Russia, to not allow Russia to remain a superpower, but to turn Russia into a raw materials producing, Third World country. They implemented the shock therapy in Russia which in three years—from 1991 to 1994—diminished the industrial capacity of Russia to one-third its previous size.

The British and the U.S. neo-cons applied the same policy to the eastern part of Germany, which led to complete devastation—privatization, and depopulation of towns. Young women would go to the West; you had towns that had only old people. Naturally, a lot of economic anxieties went with it. It was that effect of the neo-liberal shock therapy applied to East Germany that people sensed very much as an injustice; they felt sidelined. So you have cities in East Germany that are very nice looking now because historic buildings have been restored, but if you look behind these nice facades, you see a lot of misery and a lot of disappointment. That is

USNS Comfort *hospital ship was deployed to Puerto Rico.*

why the refugee crisis hit so badly; that is why people in the East felt so much more threatened by the incoming refugees. They felt that these refugees would get things of which they were deprived.

I am saying this to remind you that it's not just the United States that is in a terrible economic situation, but the entire liberal paradigm that has resulted in all of these dramatic changes is what is still at work. I have said many times—I said it after the Brexit, I said it after the Trump vote—that this injustice will cause similar earthquakes until the injustice is remedied and replaced by a New Paradigm.

So, I think we are at an absolute crossroads, where the principles which were at the core of the American System, especially with respect to foreign policy as expressed by John Quincy Adams, are so important. This goes back even further in history to the principles of the Peace of Westphalia—that foreign policy has to be in the interest of the other, and this must be the basis for any dealings with other countries.

Right now with President Trump, you have a possibility that the United States may go back to this policy. President Trump is trying his best; he's doing it, but he's being disoriented because you have a lot of faction fights in the administration, and it's not a settled question. But *everything* depends upon the United States joining hands with Russia and China at this point, and if these three countries were to get together, there is absolutely nothing, no problem, which could not be solved.

Let's use the time between now and November to get this kind of mobilization in the United States and internationally, to get our countries on the course of joining with the New Silk Road and the new paradigm. The new paradigm is the idea that you put mankind first, the interests of humanity first, and then national interests—and that you stop thinking in geopolitical terms altogether. I'm absolutely convinced—and this has been the basis of the Schiller Institute, from the time of its founding—that if we do not change our foreign policy to such an approach, then the danger of the elimination of mankind through thermonuclear war is very high as a risk.

We have right now an incredible moment of history, and I want you to really grasp this moment, and let's move mountains.

Dennis Speed: Right now we have a situation in which Puerto Rico has been devastated, and Haiti is about to receive, assuming this all works, perhaps $30 billion from the Chinese, to rebuild Haiti—I think $4.7 billion for the city of Port-au-Prince. Now, if you look at a map and you look at the Caribbean, these two populations, which have been some of the most oppressed—Haiti being the poorest in the Western Hemisphere—could be the basis of the kind of collaboration between the United States and China.

But there is a problem, and here's what I want you to address: The people who have been activists on these things for many years, are basically really mad. They're all enraged because of the racism and the other things that they've experienced. And so, when it comes to the moment of opportunity, what they will often do is introduce another list of denunciations, whether it's of Trump or whoever, instead of realizing that the opportunity to change all this is right in front of them.

Can say something on the issue of the poetic mentality, and about being able to get beyond the rage, to see an opportunity and to calmly grasp it and to move history ahead?

Bitterness Is Denial of Self-Worth

Zepp-LaRouche: I think only in moments of extraordinary crisis can you really change history, because when everything is calm and steady then people don't feel compelled to even consider that they should change something. But when you have real tragedy striking, or an absolute disaster, then you can change. We saw this in Texas, you're seeing it in Puerto Rico. We saw it, for example, in 1945 in Germany, when people started to realize that you had to go for fundamental values, to make sure that catastrophes cannot happen again—only then do you find people willing to change. I want to quote Albert Einstein, who said, you can never solve a problem with the method of thinking which caused the problem.

Puerto Rico should never have been in such a poor condition, and we saw what the Obama administration did in terms of putting debt on the state, creating a control board, imposing austerity. Puerto Rico is part of the United States! And people should be proud that this is a moment to change it.

Now, people have forgotten what a crash program is, and I can see this in Germany. When they repair a highway or some train, it takes them months and years, and they're so slow, it's almost like manual work. When the Chinese build something, they're doing it at an absolutely unbelievable speed. And Mr. Bannon is so wrong when he says the Chinese need to steal American technology to incorporate into their own economy. Maybe this was true in the early part of its industrialization, but China has moved—for a long time now—to a completely different idea. It wants to be number one in terms of technologies; it employs the concept of leapfrogging. It puts total emphasis on the excellence of the education of its young people.

They're building railroads in half a year! I was in Lanzhou, in Dunhuang, two years ago, and I saw how they were building a railroad from Lanzhou all the way to Xinjiang in half a year. How did they do it? They didn't continuously construct it, one piece after the other, but they built it in many places at the same time. That approach Americans can do, absolutely, but it's just that they have forgotten that kind of crash program.

We have lived through the paradigm of the last 50 years, one that we have identified many times, beginning with the assassination of John F. Kennedy and the cover-up of the assassination. People have forgotten what it means to be an American. In a similar way, the Germans have forgotten what the German method of effectiveness was, because their minds have been taken over by the green ideology, to the point that nothing functions any more, in the economy or otherwise.

People have to recover their sense of vision. Imagine that the crash program can be done like the Apollo

NASA

Mission Operations Control Room on July 24, 1969, celebrating the successful conclusion of the Apollo 11 lunar landing mission, reflecting American optimism of the time.

program or the Tennessee Valley Authority program of FDR, the New Deal. Americans have reference points in your history where that has been done. And I think what is necessary is to evoke, in this moment of crisis, love for your fellow citizens and love for mankind. We are at a watershed, where an old epoch is just ending, an old epoch which was associated with the paradigm of imperialism, colonialism, geopolitics, and world wars. That epoch is potentially coming to an end, *if* we get the United States and the European nations to join hands in the Belt and Road Initiative and apply the American System to the present situation—which is really what the Chinese are doing.

As to the subjective factor: Don't go about your business as usual. Just feel a tremendous love for humanity, that we cannot tolerate that mankind should remain in its present miserable condition. You have an opium epidemic, you have a drug epidemic, you have all these problems, and the only way you can solve it is by rising above it and feeling a tremendous compassion. And then you will not tolerate the present condition, but you will have a tremendous desire to change it.

JANUARY 22, 1997

Return to the Machine-Tool Principle

by Lyndon H. LaRouche, Jr.

In science, and in history, the delusions of blind faith in "simply self-evident facts," exist only in the minds of the brutishly illiterate and the sophists. True facts, like highways, do not exist in empty space; the first step toward truth may be the recognition that roads, rather than existing as "self-evident facts," may be represented, inadequately, as situated within a well-defined physical geography. In truth, today, roads, and railroads, like shipping lanes, and all other artifacts, are selected, developed, and used, by mankind as part of a *physical-economic* geography, including the physical-economy of warfare: in truth, as parts of corridors essential, for the efficient linking of nodal points of a national, and world economy.

Similarly, machine tools come into existence, and are used, as expressions of an historically situated phase of world and national processes of economic, cultural, and demographic development. In economy, nothing, including a machine-tool, can be competently defined as a fact, without first situating its existence within that functionally historical setting in the course of which it appears, and is later superseded by a better one. This principle of scientific method was identified by Gott-

NASA

Astronaut "Gus" Grissom demonstrates the two-man spacecraft "Gemini" to President John F. Kennedy.

fried Leibniz by such rubrics as "Analysis Situs."[1]

Nothing competent can be said about any aspect of economic, political, and cultural problems today, without first stating the following. We proceed thus here.

Analysis Situs: Since the middle of the 1960s, an accelerating, fundamental, downward trend in economic policy, has dominated the economies of the U.S.A., western Europe, and international relations generally.

---

1. See "Studies in a Geometry of Situation," in ***Gottfried Wilhelm Leibniz: Philosophical Papers and Letters***, Leroy E. Leomker, ed., Second Edition (Dodrecht, Netherlands: Kluwer Academic Publishers, 1989); pp. 248-258. The Leibniz ***Monadology*** should also be read as a text on the subject of *Analysis Situs*.

Analysis Situs: In the setting of the new "balance of power agreements" emerging in the aftermath of the 1962 "Cuba Missiles Crisis," and of the November 1963 assassination of U.S. President John F. Kennedy, leading oligarchical family circles, in the United States and western Europe, assumed that there was no longer a danger of general nuclear warfare among the principal powers, but only diplomatically managed, "limited wars," including "international terrorism." Thus, leading circles among these wealthy oligarchical families, assumed, that, for the medium and long term, there was no foreseeable strategic need to continue the institution of the modern sovereign nation-state, or the form of agro-industrial policies associated with that form of nation-state.

Thus, again, *Analysis Situs*: The U.S.A. economy, and the world's, was shifted, at an accelerating rate, to a policy of fostering "neo-Malthusian," "post-industrial" utopianism, away from the commitment which had characterized all our republic's economic and cultural successes, from our first war against the British monarchy, 1776-1783, until the mid-1960s: increasing the productive powers of labor through *strategic* investment in scientific and technological progress.

Under this regime (*Analysis Situs*), about 1966, this shift in policy was spread from the disastrous Prime Minister Harold Wilson's United Kingdom, into the United States, and also into the western European continent. The first neo-Malthusian policy was introduced into the U.S. State Department about 1966. It arrived in the U.S., domestic, economic policy, during 1966-1967, as the first of a series of massive cut-backs in the space program.

An accelerating contraction in the economy followed such 1966-67 policy-shifts, leading into the Chrysler and Penn Central bankruptcies of 1970, and the "Henry A. Kissinger administration's" August 1971 take-down of the pre-existing Bretton Woods agreements. As a continuation of this plunge into "post-industrial" utopianism, we experienced the 1971-1972 shift, from a system of stable international monetary relations, into the speculators' lunacy of a "floating exchange-rate" system. President Jimmy Carter's October 1979 appointment of Paul A. Volcker as Federal Reserve chairman, completed the principal policy-changes under whose guidance we are plunging into national bankruptcy today.

Consequently, as these things must be measured in physical content of market-baskets, the income and output of the U.S. labor-force, per capita, has fallen, today, to approximately half what it was a quarter-century earlier.[2] Hence, as shown in earlier issues of *EIR*: commonly, a U.S. household in the lower ninety percent of income-ranges, requires two to three incomes today, to attempt to reach the real-income standard achieved by households with one, or one-and-a-half incomes a quarter-century earlier.[3] Similar results prevail in western Europe, with worse results in eastern Europe and the former Soviet Union. The collapse prevailing throughout the developing sector as a whole, has been worse. The condition of sub-Sahara Africa has been unspeakable, and no national economy of Central and South America has failed to degenerate, consistently, during the entire twenty-five year period, especially since the beginning of 1982.

In fact, as measured in physical-economic market-baskets of purchasing power, the U.S. economy has contracted by more than 2% per annum each year since 1971. The false, contrary claims, by some agencies of the U.S. Government, and other quotable authorities, have been premised chiefly upon two general classes of fallacy in reporting. First, a mixture of wishful incompetence in choice of statistical yardsticks, combined with naked, politically motivated outright statistical frauds by the Federal Reserve and other relevant agencies. Second, failing to take into account, imputable, unpaid costs, such as unrepaid attrition in previously constructed, essential economic infrastructure, combined with attrition in capital elements, such as machine-tool capabilities.

Take the case of the recent, disastrous floods in northern California, for which the blame lies, not with the weather, but the breakdown of over-aged flood-control infrastructure. The responsibility lies with those who made the decisions, during the past thirty years, to the present day, not to maintain the flood control sys-

2. This includes not only physical goods as such, but also those forms of education, health-care, and science services (such as fundamental research) which are essential to fostering the per-capita cognitive potential of the population for current and future levels of scientific and technological progress in designs of products and productive processes. It includes not only household consumption, but also infrastructure, agriculture, mining, and industry. See discussion of this principle of economic measurement, under the rubric of "*Analysis Situs* in econometrics," below.

3. See Christopher White, "NAM's 'Renaissance' of U.S. Industry: It Never Happened," *EIR*, April 14, 1995; *EIR Special Report*: "U.S. Consumer Market Basket Shrinks to the Crisis Point," *EIR*, Sept. 27, 1996.

tems which had been designed and constructed to prevent precisely such a catastrophe. Consider the cumulative deadly, or otherwise grave implications of a collapse of the nation's power or railway systems, and deregulation-caused collapses within the U.S. airline industry.

Consider the impact of the irrational shift in U.S. national policy of practice, away from inland waterways and rails, to that greatly excessive reliance upon costly highway transport, which has been the long-term, ruinous trend in the U.S. economy throughout the 1945-1996 interval.[4] The U.S. Army Corps of Engineers' estimates coincide with results of independent, late 1970s, studies made by the Fusion Energy Foundation. In terms of energy costs per ton of bulk freight, rail transport is only 40% as economical as inland waterways, while truck transport is merely 30% as efficient as rail. Economic efficiency depends crucially upon increasing steadily the number, and relative cheapness, of kilowatt-hours available per household, and, even more emphatically, to agriculture and industry. In production, efficiency depends upon increasing the applied energy-flux-density of power, and the relative coherence of that application, per operative.

General economic efficiency depends upon maintaining increasing percentiles, over 90%, of the total population within well-maintained cities, as opposed to the vastly wasteful correlation of growth of "suburbanization" and urban slums, during the recent forty-five-odd years. The breakdown of the cities, has driven people into suburbs, with the resulting costs in time and money to households (and costs to national, state, and local governmental agencies) incurred through commuting, and also as the social costs of breakdown in family life, including the increase in crime-rates: all caused, in large part, by the costs and other burdens of commuting-time, an affliction added to the effects of an increased number of incomes required per household. As the recent thirty years' experience demonstrates, low costs of production, low-cost quality education, and

health-care, can not be provided under the combined impact of increasing suburbanization and shifts into the "neo-Malthusian, post-industrial" utopianism, and into virtual-reality fads such as "information society."

Here, we focus upon a single, characteristic feature of the recent thirty years' devolution of the world economy taken as a whole: *the crucial impact of cutting deeply into capital costs of machine-tool input, ostensibly to effect a more competitive pricing of commodities.*

These cuts have been defended, often, in the name of lowering the costs of production, through decreasing the "overhead load" attributable to research and development. Obviously, if a firm eliminates the costs associated with use of the machine-tool factor in design of product and productive processes, foolish accountants and financial managers will insist, that this is an apparent cost-saving, which renders the firm more price-competitive, and also contributes to increasing the percentile of total income distributable to shareholders.[5] What has been contemptuously, and fairly described as the "globaloney" of "out-sourcing," is one of the tricks by means of which this looting of the productivity of the U.S. economy is extended to about the same ultimate effect as driving a truck across a non-existent bridge.

In reality, contrary to the sophistries of such financial managers and accountants, the result of continuing such purported savings, is national economic bankruptcy. In reality, the continued profitability of any modern agro-industrial economy, taken as a whole, depends absolutely upon the technological increase in productive powers of the labor-force, a gain in efficiency derived almost entirely from the combination of education for scientific and technological progress, and the associated role of the kind of machine-tool sector which was built up in collaboration between Alexander Dallas Bache's United States and Alexander von Humboldt's Germany, during the Nineteenth Century. The key to understanding the impending doom of the U.S. economy under the axiomatic trends in policy-shaping which have reigned during the recent thirty years, is the catastrophic collapse of, combined, the quality of education supplied in the classroom, and the savage, accelerating reduction of the role of the machine-tool sector of the economy.

---

4. The systematic destruction of the post-World War II national transportation system, was fully under way during the 1950s, marked by the looting of the New Haven Railroad and subsequent, pre-1957 recession, failure to merge the Pennsylvania and New York Central systems. Then, under President Jimmy Carter's deregulation, came the ruin of both the national trucking and airlines systems. The proper, crucial relationship between a trucking and railroad industry, which still might have been pulled off during the second half of the 1950s, will require a protectionist program of reconstruction, and coordination of functions, of both the rail and trucking-warehousing industries.

5. Financial managers and accountants represent an essential service to the management of the productive process, a usefulness which ends, abruptly, and often disastrously, when financial executives or accountants overstep the limits of their competence, to impose the mere "virtual reality" of their crafts upon management of the productive process.

Southeast Asia: Tabbies, Not Tigers

Amid today's popular gossip of the bar-rooms and the *Wall Street Journal*, there is the delusion, that the so-called "Asian Tigers" of Southeast Asia typify the glorious future of a world in which national economies have been junked, for the supposed advantages of "global economy." Let us explore that delusion, as a way of illustrating the general factual point to be made.

The term "Asian Tigers" is often applied carelessly to three axiomatically distinct species of economies in east Asia: a) The post-1949 agro-industrial economies of Japan, South Korea, and Taiwan, which are models for what could, and must be done throughout Asia generally; b) Hongkong and Singapore, those Venice-like parasites of the Orient, whose prosperity is, in large degree, a by-product of the flow of opium from the high mountain ("Golden Triangle") regions on Thailand's and China's borders; c) The presently imperilled, superficial, mayfly exuberance of Southeast Asia's Thailand, Malaysia, and Indonesia.

See **Figure 1**, "Tigers With Teeth," prepared by *EIR*'s Asia desk. This presents the evidence, that Japan, Taiwan, and South Korea's industrial economies, as measured in U.S. dollars of machine-tool output per capita, are dominated by a machine-tool sector which puts the rapidly collapsing, relatively backward U.S., apparently, into the class of an economically half-witted poor relative.[6] Note, in this chart, the 1979-1981 turning-point, the point at which the U.S. economy began its presently accelerated phase of collapse, out of the disastrous impact of the so-called "Volcker Measures" and Gramm-Rudman "budget-balancing" lunacies.

---

6. We may leave it to the Harvard University pro-racialist "Black Studies" program, which alleged, fraudulently, the genetic Africa origins of Harvard-invented "Ebonics," to say whether the economic superiority of the Japanese, Koreans, and Chiang Kai-chek's leadership, over American "Baby Boomers," should also be seen as genetic in origin. Competent researchers know that there are no genetically determined differences in cognitive potential of individuals which can be attributed to so-called "racial" origins. There is only the issue of the right to access of all persons, of whatever so-called "ethnic" origins, to whatever are the education and employment opportunities which correspond to the most advanced levels of culture on our planet. It amuses the writer, however, to throw into the face of the racialists, at Harvard and Vanderbilt Universities, and elsewhere, in today's U.S.A., the evidence which might suggest to Harvard empiricists, that perhaps Japanese, Koreans, and Chinese are genetically superior in cognitive powers, to Harvard- or Vanderbilt-inspired economists, politicians, and literati.

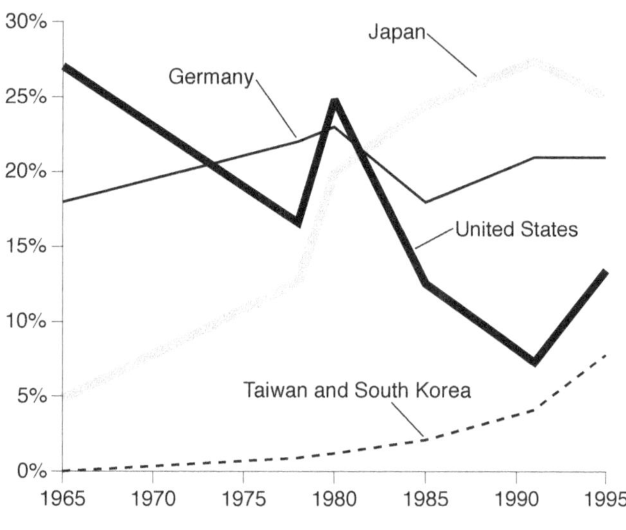

FIGURE 1

Tigers with Teeth: Percent Share of World Machine Tool Production

Source: Association for Manufacturing Technology (formerly the U.S. National Machine Tool Builders Association).

Do not classify Asia's blowfish among its tigers: Put to one side, the dangerously silly Mont Pelerin Society's choice of monetarist paradise, the non-comparable cases of the Venice-style, "hot-money" *entrepôts* of Asia, Hongkong and Singapore. Stick to the relevant cases; contrast the vast superiority of the real "Asian Tigers," of North Asia, with the "Potemkin Village" facade of prosperity, as featured in the Southeast Asia region: the Philippines, Vietnam, Kampuchea, Laos, Malaysia, Thailand, Indonesia, et al. Consider, *seriatim*, some relevant points of distinction.

The Philippines used to enjoy a significant machine-tool potential, centered upon the U.S. naval base at Subic Bay; that potential began to be destroyed, by the U.S. government and IMF, during the "Volcker years." The Philippines economy was virtually destroyed by the U.S. coup d'état which Vice-President George Bush's, mid-1980s, "secret government" organized against President Ferdinand Marcos. Much of that economic potential was simply packed up by the U.S. Government, and shipped out, leaving only the emptied hulks of the looted buildings to haunt the victimized nation's people.

Vietnam, Kampuchea, and Laos, have yet to recover from the desolation left in the wake of more than eight years of the U.S.A.'s post-Kennedy "balance of power" sports on the territory of France's old Indo-China colony. Indonesia is the best case among the remaining economies of the region; Germany's Aachen University alumnus, Professor Bachruddin Jusuf Habibie, one of the most influential figures of Indonesia's economic scene today, has led in the attempt to build a high-technology skyscraper, so to speak, from the roof down. There is a semblance—if only a semblance—of a nascent, possible future machine-tool potential there, but nothing, yet, remotely comparable to Japan, Korea, and Taiwan; otherwise, there is no presently existing basis, or competent policy for the present, or future autonomous economic development in any among the other nations of that economic tragedy known as Southeast Asia.

The "out-sourcing industries" of Thailand and Malaysia, represent a present-day parody of the economic model of foreign-controlled plantations and mining enclaves, as seen in British, Dutch, and French colonies of the late Nineteenth Century. Today's manufacturing "out-source" facility in these nations, is simply a way for foreign financial powers to loot the host-nation, through exploitation of cheap labor, in the same sense that plantations and mining enclaves were characteristics of the looting practiced by such colonial powers as Britain, the Netherlands, and France, during the late Nineteenth Century. In the "cosmopolitan centers" of that former colonial world, today, as during the late Nineteenth and early Twentieth Centuries, there is a cheap veneer, of apparent cash prosperity, featuring the fabulously decadent new rich of the "Asia hot-money" social set, with shopping and tourist entertainments to match. Behind, and underneath that "Potemkin Village" facade, the economy as a whole, is rotted out with such evils of colonial-style poverty as mass prostitution, epidemics, and a cultural pessimism redolent with a looming threat, that new Pol Pot-style rampages might soon wreak vengeance upon today's decadent rich, throughout the region.

There is a way in which the patriotic aims of Indonesia's Dr. Habibie could be realized, and the other states of Southeast Asia rescued, similarly, from their recently apparent slide toward looming catastrophe; but, that success depends absolutely upon choosing a different route than the blending of "Asia hot-money" trafficking and the lunatic sort of monetarist dogmas which have been fostered by the doomed, presently reigning international monetary and financial institutions.

Why Most Economists Are Charlatans

Behind the onrushing catastrophes of the present international monetary, financial, and economic policies, there are the bungling propagandists, those Yahoos who are called professors, those mugs who write the widely used textbooks, and who lecture the gaping-mouthed credulous students in virtually every economics classroom of the world today. Yet, some of the world's senior economists, such as the U.S.'s John Kenneth Galbraith, or France's Maurice Allais, have occasionally trumpeted insightful defiance of the "politically correct," lunatic dogmas and practices of today's classroom and foundation-sponsored lecturers. These exceptional outbursts remind us of the little boy in the Hans Christian Andersen fairy-tale, "The Emperor's New Suit of Clothes": the emperors of today's economics textbook and classroom, "have nothing on."

Gottfried Leibniz, whose work of the 1671-1716 interval is the foundation of economic science, still today, supplies the key to the occurrence of such paradoxical flashes of competence from amid the horde of deranged hesychasts dominating today's economics classroom.[7] The term which Leibniz used to identify that point of difference between the, usual, academic quack, and the, rarer, insightful economic thinker, is that we cited at the outset, here: *Analysis Situs*. This references those fundamental principles of scientific method, earlier used by Plato, Leonardo da Vinci, and Johannes Kepler, which stand outside, and above the domain of all today's generally accepted classroom dogmas of deductive mathematics.

This notion of *Analysis Situs* is crucial for understanding the machine-tool principle. We now proceed with the outlining of that prerequisite conception.

In the past, the present author has, repeatedly, re-introduced two charts into sundry published locations.[8]

---

7. See Lyndon H. LaRouche, Jr., *So, You Wish to Learn All About Economics?*, Second Edition (Washington, D.C.: EIR News Service, 1995). Essential features of Leibniz's 1671-1716 development of the science of physical economy were incorporated in the anti-Locke U.S. 1776 Declaration of Independence and the 1787-1789 drafting of the anti-Locke U.S. Federal Constitution. Although *the American System of political-economy* of U.S. founder Benjamin Franklin, U.S. Treasury Secretary Alexander Hamilton, Matthew Carey, Henry C. Carey, the Henry Clay Whigs, President John Quincy Adams, and Germany's Friedrich List is consistent with the anti-empiricist principles of Leibniz's science, the revival of that science itself waited until the present author's original discoveries from the period 1948-1952. The core of those 1948-1952 discoveries is explicitly referenced here.

8. For example: Lyndon H. LaRouche, Jr., "Leibniz From Riemann's

Growth of European Population, Population-density, and Life-expectancy at Birth, Estimated for 100,000 B.C.–A.D. 1975.

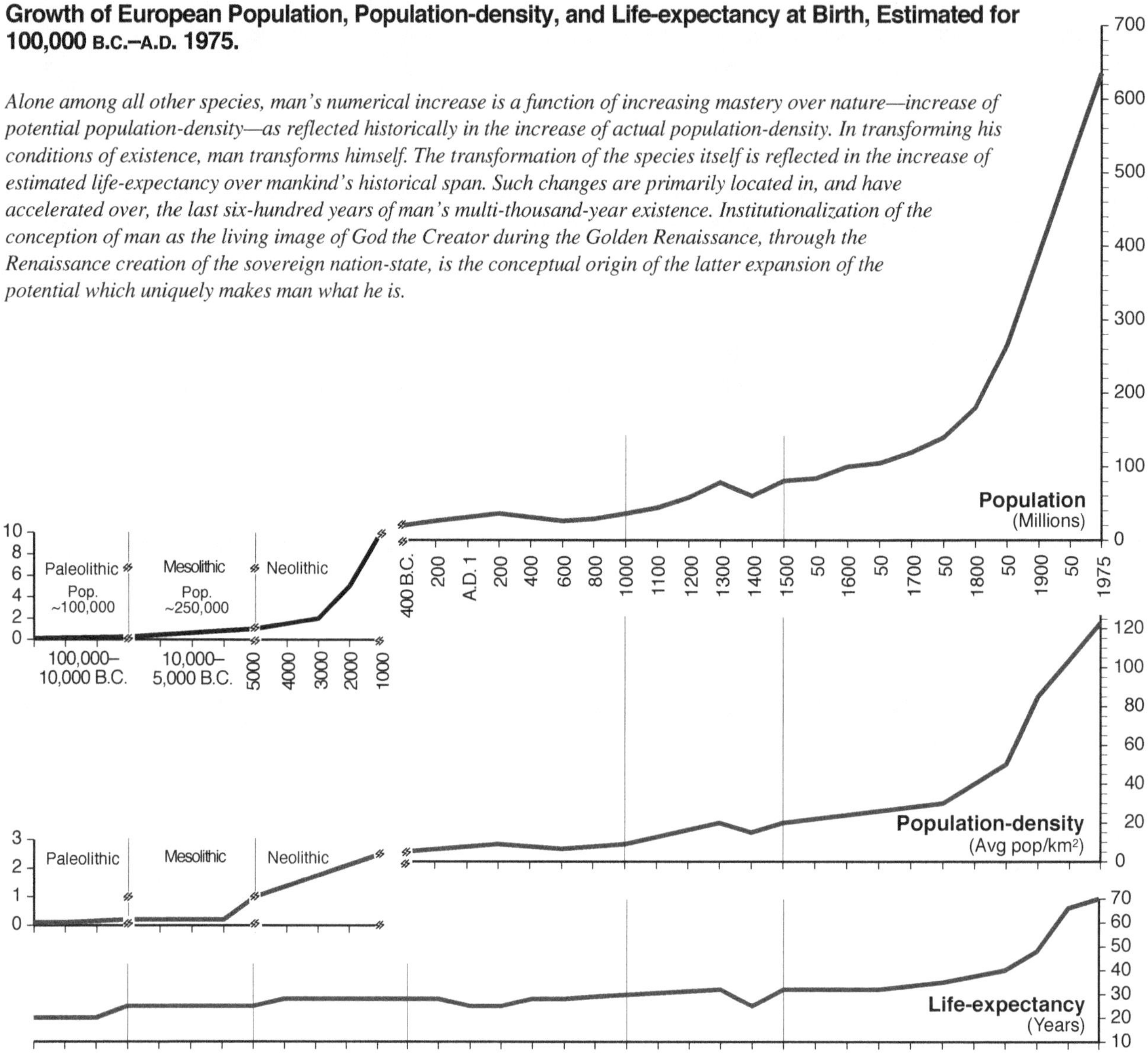

Alone among all other species, man's numerical increase is a function of increasing mastery over nature—increase of potential population-density—as reflected historically in the increase of actual population-density. In transforming his conditions of existence, man transforms himself. The transformation of the species itself is reflected in the increase of estimated life-expectancy over mankind's historical span. Such changes are primarily located in, and have accelerated over, the last six-hundred years of man's multi-thousand-year existence. Institutionalization of the conception of man as the living image of God the Creator during the Golden Renaissance, through the Renaissance creation of the sovereign nation-state, is the conceptual origin of the latter expansion of the potential which uniquely makes man what he is.

All charts are based on standard estimates compiled by existing schools of demography. None claim any more precision than the indicative; however, the scaling flattens out what might otherwise be locally, or even temporally, significant variation, reducing all thereby to the set of changes which is significant, independant of the quality of estimates and scaling of the graphs. Sources: For population and population-density, Colin McEvedy and Richard Jones, *Atlas of World Population History*; for life-expectancy, various studies in historical demography.

Note breaks and changes in scales.

The first of these, reintroduced here as **Figure 2**, is entitled "Growth of European Population, Population Density, and Life-Expectancy at Birth, Estimated for 100,000 B.C.-A.D. 1975." The second, reintroduced here as **Table 1**, is entitled "Development of Human Population, from Recent Research Estimates," covering evidence from the period 4,000,000-1,000,000 B.C.

Standpoint," *Fidelio*, Fall 1996, pp. 37-38.

through A.D. 1970. There might be some improvement in the precision of the figures supplied by the present-day experts, but there is no possible rational objection to the representation of the orders of magnitude, and of shifts in the curve of improvement of the demographic characteristics of populations.

Both sets of demographic data are essential to providing clarity for the crucial point to be made here. However, that noted, the immediately relevant of the two fig-

Development of Human Population, from Recent Research Estimates

	Life expectancy at birth (years)		Population density (per km2)	Comments	World population (millions)
Primate Comparison					
Gorilla			1/km2		.07
Chimpanzee			3-4/km2		1+
Man					
Australopithecines B.C. 4,000,000-1,000,000		14-15	1/ 10 km2	68% die by age 14	.07-1
Homo Erectus B.C. 900,000-400,000		14-15			1.7
Paleolithic (hunter-gatherers) B.C. 100,000-15,000		18-20+	1/ 10 km2	55% die by age 14; average age 23	
Mesolithic (proto-agricultural) B.C. 15,000-5,000		20-27			4
Neolithic, B.C. 10,000-3,000		25	1/km2	"Agricultural revolution"	10
Bronze Age B.C. 3,000-1,000		28	10/km2	50% die by age 14 Village dry-farming, Baluchistan, 5,000 B.C.: 9.61/km2 Development of cities: Sumer, 2000 B.C.: 19.16/km2 Early Bronze Age: Aegean, 3,000 B.C.: 7.5-13.8/km2 Late Bronze Age: Aegean, 1,000 B.C.: 12.4-31.3/km2 Shang Dynasty China, 1000 B.C.: 5/km2	50
Iron Age, B.C. 1,000-		28			50

Mediterranean Classical Period B.C. 500-A.D. 500		25-28	15+/km2	Classical Greece, Peloponnese: 35/km2
				Roman Empire:
				  Greece: 11/km2 Italy: 24/km2
				  Asia: 30/km2 Egypt: 179/km2*
				Han Dynasty China, B.C. 200-A.D. 200: 19.27/km2
				  Shanxi: 28/km2 Shaanxi: 24/km2
				  Henan: 97/km2* Shandong: 118/km2*
				* Irrigated river-valley intensive agriculture
					100-190

European Medieval Period A.D. 800-1300		30+	20+/km2	40% die by age 14 Italy, 1200: 24/km2 Italy, 1340: 34/km2 Tuscany, 1340: 85/km2 Brabant, 1374: 35/km2	220-360
Europe, 17th Century		32-36		Italy, 1650: 37/km2 France, 1650: 38/km2 Belgium, 1650: 50/km2	545
Europe, 18th Century		34-38	30+/km2	"Industrial Revolution" Italy, 1750: 50/km2 France, 1750: 44/km2 Belgium, 1750: 108/km2	720
Massachusetts, 1840		41	90+/km2	Life expectancies: "Industrialized," right; "Pre-industrialized," left	1,200
United Kingdom, 1861		43			
Guatemala, 1893	24				
European Russia, 1896	32				
Czechoslovakia, 1900		40			
Japan, 1899		44			
United States, 1900		48			
Sweden, 1903		53			
France, 1946		62			
India, 1950	41				2,500
Sweden, 1960		73			
1970			**1975**		3,900
United States		71	26/km2		
West Germany		70	248/km2		
Japan		73	297/km2		
China	59		180/km2		
India	48		183/km2		
Belgium			333/km2		

ures, is the unprecedented rate of improvements of the demographic characteristics of the entire population of this planet, over the period which began with the 1439-1440 sessions of the Council of Florence, and the consequent establishment of the first modern nation-state, Louis XI's France, until that downturn in conditions of life, the which began with the mid-1960s introduction of the neo-Malthusian cult of anti-scientific, "post-industrial" utopianism. It is the secret of the modern nation-state's incomparable, 1471-1966 achievements, in improvement of the demographic characteristics of life, and cultural standard of living, throughout nearly all of this planet, which generated the later role of the machine-tool principle as the dominant feature of leading instances of successful performance among the Ninteenth and Twentieth Centuries' political economies.

The crux of the matter, is the inextricable interdependency among: 1) the spread of a Classical humanist mode of universal cognitive education, extended, as compulsory under the authority of the state, for all young persons;[9] 2) the fostering, by the same state, of both development of basic economic infrastructure and fostering of investment in increase of the productive powers of labor through capital-intensive, power-intensive modes of scientific and technological progress;[10] 3) the

transmission of discovered principles of nature from experimental science and Classical humanist education, to the design of products and processes of production, through the mediation of what is sometimes identified as the "strategic" component of the machine-tool sector. This interdependency emerged to become a characteristic feature of the most successful national cultures, as part of the spread of the institution of the modern European mode of sovereign nation-state, since that new institution's appearance in France and elsewhere, following the A.D. 1439-1440 sessions of the "Golden Renaissance's" great ecumenical Council of Florence.

In earlier locations, the author and his associates have examined the pre-history and history of the Fifteenth-Century emergence and development of the modern, European model of sovereign nation-state. We have shown that that process of emergence reflects the central feature of human history: which earlier pre-history and history yearned toward, and by which all present and subsequent history must be judged. The central, axiomatic feature, which sets the modern sovereign form of nation-state apart from, and above, all earlier and contrastable forms of society, is the axiomatic authority over statecraft, attributed to the Mosaic principle of *Genesis* 1, that man and woman are each made, alike, in the image of the Creator, that our species might exert domination over nature as a whole.

This axiomatic, Mosaic principle is situated, for the notions of both natural law and general practices of statecraft, within the scientific principle of "simultaneity of all."[11] That, although each mortal life appears within the passage of time, carrying on the work of predecessors, and building the foundation for the future, that work which the mortal individual does, during the brief passage through mortal life, must be judged for its service to the heritage of all past, present, and future humanity.

For the purposes of statecraft, and the application of natural law to statecraft, the goal of statecraft is to foster the benefit, expressable as our Constitution's notion of "general welfare … to ourselves and our posterity," of fostering the development and work of persons who are encouraged and assisted to become as men and women of Providence, individuals whose coming, from birth to

---

9. The modern type of Classical humanist education is exemplified by the program of humanist secondary education, rooted in the principles of Friedrich Schiller, which Schiller's student, Wilhelm von Humboldt, established as the Classical secondary educational program of modern Germany (before and after Hitler, until this educational program was destroyed by the so-called Brandt reforms). The distinctive functional feature of such forms of education, is emphasis upon the student's reenacting key valid discoveries of principle within the sovereign precincts of the individual mind, as opposed to so-called "textbook," or presently updated versions of the old "blab school" pedagogy. Humboldt's is also the model for the system of Classical high-school education established in the United States, by Benjamin Franklin's great-grandson, the collaborator of Carl F. Gauss and Alexander von Humboldt (Whilhelm's brother), Alexander Dallas Bache. This mode of education, is to be seen as opposed to the "blab school" tradition of Professor Newton "Eisenbart" Gingrich, which has taken over U.S. education since the mid-1960s. It takes its roots from the Platonic tradition of the medieval and modern Christian teaching orders, such as the Brothers of the Common Life.

10. On the subject of the measurement of what Leibniz and his followers, such as U.S. Treasury Secretary Alexander Hamilton, identify as "increase of the productive powers of labor," see LaRouche, op cit. Productive power of labor, is to be measured in terms of a characteristic potential relative population-density of a society at a certain level of sustained cultural development: e.g., in a sense analogous to the classroom notion of "energy of the system." This is measured, approximately, in terms of input and output 1) per capita, of labor-force, in 2) per square kilometer of relevant land-area. On Hamilton's views, see his December 1791 *Report to the U.S. Congress: On The Subject of Man-*

ufactures; see Nancy Spannaus & Christopher White, *The Political Economy of the American Revolution*, second edition (Washington, D.C.: *Executive Intelligence Review*, 1995). pp. ix-49, 390-454.

11. On the relativity of time, see Lyndon H. LaRouche, Jr., "The Essential Role of 'Time-Reversal' in Mathematical Economics," *EIR*, Oct. 11, 1996.

death, is as the passage of a stranger among us, a stranger whose passing-through may be regarded as a blessing afforded by the Hand of Providence.

This potential for good, which is inborn in all human individuals, is that power of reason which sets the human species absolutely apart from, and above all beasts, a power expressed as the capacity to discover valid principles of nature, principles which each over-turn all previously established opinions. Knowledge of these principles, may be passed from one individual, to another, not as intellectually sterile, linear "information," but, rather, by a cognitive process fairly described as reenactment of the original mental act of discovery.

That "non-informational," cognitive discovery and transmission, is the sole means by which mankind is en-abled to increase its power over nature, as that increase is expressed in terms of the notion, that potential relative population-density is measured not only in terms of population-density, but in standard of cultural life per capita, and per household, throughout that society as a whole. It is precisely here, that we must locate the indis-pensable interrelationship among Classical humanist forms of education, the development of the machine-tool sector, and the production of a labor-force which is capable, generally, of assimilating, and projecting the progress mediated through the machine-tool sector.

Thus, the essence of that Fifteenth-Century found-ing of the modern nation-state, is, that, for the first time in all earlier political history of peoples of this planet, the generality of individual personalities was elevated from the status of subject, to citizen, this according to an *axiomatic principle*. That axiom is, that society must be constituted and self-governed according to the famous principle of ***Genesis*** 1: that man and woman are made in the image of the Creator, set above the beasts to the effect that mankind must effect dominion over nature and the beasts through the nurture and employ-ment of that unique, cognitive distinction, of potential for valid, original discoveries of principle, through cre-ative reason, which is common to newborn human indi-viduals.

That principle is the only basis for rational use of the term "equal" respecting a universality of individual persons; that principle is a kind of "modulus," in Gauss's sense of that term for both common and higher arithmetic, which measures, the commonality—the congruence, of persons, as members of a species, as a quality which underlies their differences as individuals.

This commonality is the political equality of each and all persons. The right which the individual person must enjoy, is not, as the immoral empiricists argue today, the right of a passing majority to impose its ca-pricious opinions, tyrannically, upon the minority. That perverted notion of a "democracy" of mere opinions, is the mother of all tyrannies, including those horrid dic-tatorships which are spawned by the characteristic ex-cesses to which democratic arbitrariness is prone. The modern nation-state's durability depends upon a peo-ple's submission to those certain immutable principles of universal law, the which take into account the rights of the future generations of citizens, with even greater emphasis than those of the presently living ones. It is the kind of immutable, constitutional principle of law, in which the right granted, by such law, to the individ-ual person, must be defended even contrary to the opin-ion of an overwhelming political majority. Without a nation under such law, rather than under the capri-ciously passing whims of accidental majorities, no person has, in fact, any rights at all.

Without the existence and enforcement of such law, the clock is turned back to the great gambling casino of law called barbarism, in which the individual is subject to the inherently capricious perversities of decisions issued for the convenience of the reigning imperial Pontifex Maximus, as conditioned only by the tyrant's cautious concern to avoid the appearance of offending too loudly, not law, but the current opinion of mere reli-gious and other custom among the victims of the impe-rial will.[12]

The axiomatic principle to which we have referred, thus, is not to be deprecated as "merely" some specific religious body's arbitrary choice of ethic; it is a demon-strable principle of experimental physical science, a principle characteristic of known human pre-history and history, in the sense that Plato, Leonardo da Vinci, Jo-hannes Kepler, Gottfried Leibniz, Carl F. Gauss, and Bernhard Riemann, among others, understood the prin-ciple of experimental physical science. Figures 2 and 3 illustrate the nature of the physical evidence to this effect. The raw beginning of the experimental-physics argument to this effect, is, that the combination, of in-creases in potential relative population-density, and im-provement of demogaphic characteristics of populations

---

12. For the view of the revolutionary moral impact of the modern na-tion-state, over morally inferior earlier forms of culture, see Friedrich von der Heydte, ***Die Geburtsstunde des Souveraenen Staates*** (Regens-burg, Germany: Druck und Verlag Josef Habbel, 1952).

Adam Smith (1723-90)   *Karl Marx (1818-83)*   *Leonhard Euler (1707-83)*

and their households, is the product of a voluntary principle of man's willful, cognitive (not "informational") dominion over nature, absent in all lower forms of life.

The notion of man and woman as each made in the image of the Creator, is, in short, like the legendary principle of gravity, a universal principle of natural law, to which all nations, peoples, and persons are equally subject, a principle which they may violate only at natural risk, whether they choose to recognize its authority, or not. Thus, is true law situated, as it must be located in the simultaneity of all: *Analysis Situs*, yet once more; so, the leaders in the creation of the young American republic of 1776-1789, followers of Leibniz, and adversaries of the pro-slavery John Locke on precisely these accounts, framed a Declaration of Independence which features "Life, liberty, and the pursuit of happiness," Leibniz's rejoinder against Locke, in preference to the slave-holder's and Confederate sophistry of "Life, liberty, and property." So, the Leibnizian notion of "general welfare" came to be featured as integral to the fundamental law of our Federal Republic, the Preamble of its Constitution.

To understand the causes for the inevitable, onrushing doom of the world's present international monetary and financial institutions, we must examine the present-day issues of generally taught economics from the vantage-point just stated. It is the generally accepted philosophies of economic and related social policy, of today's university classrooms, the which represent the axiomatic root of the galloping moral and intellectual decadence, and onrushing doom, of the U.S.A.'s and the world's economy today.

That axiomatic issue is the irreconcilable difference between two irreconcilably opposing conceptions of the individual personality. On the one side, the notion associated with Plato and Christianity, the principle strongly affirmed by the founding of the Golden Renaissance: the principle, that man and woman are each made in the image of God, to exert increasing dominion over nature. The opposing principle, is the mechanistic notion of man, as a talking beast. This mechanistic perversion is the characteristic of all thought properly filed under the rubric "Enlightenment": its (empiricist, materialist, logical positivist) dogmas in history, economics, political science generally, and modern empiricist and positivist teachings of anthropology, sociology, psychology, and even mathematics.[13] This is the dogma of the followers of the neo-Aristoteleans William of Ockham and Pietro Pomponazzi, led by Paolo Sarpi, and such among Sarpi's lackeys and followers as Galileo Galilei, Francis Bacon, Thomas Hobbes, John Locke, Bernard Mandeville, the feudalist Dr. François Quesnay, Voltaire, Adam Smith, Leonhard Euler, Jeremy Bentham, Immanuel Kant, and so on.

In political-economy, the Enlightenment's bestialized misconception of individual human nature, is the universal characteristic of every "main scream" economics and related teaching today. *To wit*:

The crucial point of departure for the present writer's crucial, original, 1948-1952 discoveries of princi-

____

13. On mathematics, see below.

ple in the science of physical economy, was a simultaneous attack on the characteristic fallacy of Marx's economics as well as the "information theory" hoax of Norbert Wiener and the perversion called "systems analysis," as typified by Wiener's associate John von Neumann.

Just as Marx insists, in sundry locations within his four-volume *Capital*: in constructing his deterministic model of capitalist reproduction, he has left technological progress out of account. Marx ignores all of the then available authorities in economic science, to follow in the footsteps of the authorities from which he, aided by British foreign intelligence's David Urquhart, selected his grounding in economics. Marx based himself on the previous arguments of Enlightenment ideologues such as François Quesnay, Giammaria Ortes, Adam Smith, and David Ricardo. Despite Marx's occasional differences with these wretched predecessors, he never departed from those crucial fallacious axiomatic assumptions of the Enlightenment, the which he shared in common with all of them, from Hobbes through John Stuart Mill, Bertrand Russell, and John von Neumann. Thus, as relevant figures from among leading figures of both Britain's Cambridge "Systems Analysis" circles, and Soviet specialists, observed, it is quite feasible to freely substitute Marx, or Leon Walras, or John Maynard Keynes, or the mathematical constructs of von Neumann, for one another in the same recipe for servings of academic economics stew. No such model actually works, but, to whatever passes for the taste-buds of the department's relevant virtual-reality center, the computer, they all share in common the same permeating flavor of *papier-mâché*.

As Cambridge University's Piero Sraffa sums the matter up, in his 1960 ***The Production of Commodities by Commodities***, all of today's generally accepted, formalist representations of academic economic dogma, can be reduced to the assumption that some correlation between the abstract inputs and outputs of a system of simultaneous linear inequalities, can be stated for either prices or some other scalar metric, without considering the possibility that some determining sort of functional relationship exists between cognitive powers of the operative's mind, and variation in the qualities of product and productive powers of labor. Just as mathematician Thomas Hobbes' model of society anticipates a crude approximation of Ludwig Boltzmann's mathematical model for any unpleasantly aromatic collection of gas-particles, so, all other generally accepted attempts at deterministic, academic models of economy, Adam Smith's concoction and others, degrade man to a mere colligation of interacting, sinful appetites.

Thus, Norbert Wiener represents societies by reference to Boltzmann's H-theorem. So, John von Neumann constructed his economic models of systems analysis, and professed to have redesigned the human mind, by "retro-fitting" it with those qualities of "artificial intelligence" which would bring psychology into less imperfect conformity with Thomas Hobbes' perversions, and von Neumann's own.

Notably, the civilian side of the Soviet economy tended toward the entropic perfection of Marx's and von Neumann's models, of solutions for sets of simultaneous linear inequalities; as we have witnessed since *perestroika* was introduced, only the substitution of Adam Smith for Marx could produce a worse result. However, in the actual practice of the Soviet military-industrial complex, we find a far less entropic model of economic behavior, a model, densely echoing the role of the machine-tool-design sector of the pre-1966 U.S.A. and German economy. The ability of the Soviet economy to challenge the military technological capabilities of the combined force of the U.S.A. and its allies for as long as it did, is reflected in the high density of scientists and engineers in the Soviet economy's strategic "machine-tool design" sector. The contrast of the advanced technology of the Soviet military sector with the dismal performance of the more technologically stagnant civilian-goods sector, highlights the role of the machine-tool sector within the military economy.

The same pattern is found among the Soviets' former adversaries. During the Twentieth Century, most emphatically, the U.S. economy has been in either an embittering recession or depression during all periods except those of large-scale, pre-war or war-time military mobilization. A related pattern has always been characteristic of the British Empire, since about the time of the 1714 accession of William of Orange's tamed Welf, George I, to the throne. So, also, in western continental Europe.

How To Measure Economic Performance

As this author has elaborated his 1948-52 original discoveries in economic science in numerous earlier *EIR* and other locations,[14] the specific difference between human beings and apes, is the ability of the

14. e.g., Lyndon H. LaRouche, Jr., "The Essential Role of Time Reversal' in Mathematical Economics," **Fidelio** Winter 1996 (also, **EIR**, Oct. 11, 1996).

human individual to generate valid *metaphors*: ideas which have no possible existence in language as presently used, but which nonetheless represent efficient principles of our universe. Thus, any artistic work, in any medium, is not truly art except as it meets that standard of metaphor. In Classical science, since Plato's founding of his Academy at Athens, all scientific ideas come into existence as human knowledge, through this process of metaphor.

To sum up those accounts, very briefly, here: This principle of metaphor came under systematic scrutiny by Leibniz. The present author came to understand this principle during mid-adolescence, through study of Leibniz's attacks on Descartes, his writings in the Leibniz-Clarke correspondence, and the Leibniz writing published under the title of **The Monadology**. It was chiefly through the present author's late-adolescent elaboration of a rigorous defense of Leibniz's **Monadology**, against the attack featured within I. Kant's **Critique of Pure Reason**, that this writer was prepared, a decade later, to attack the fraud of neo-Kantian Norbert Wiener's "information theory." The result of this assault against Wiener's and John von Neumann's systems-analysis hoaxes, produced the writer's 1948-1951 original discoveries concerning the relationship between the individual's metaphor-generating, sovereign cognitive processes and the gains in productive powers of labor through scientific progress. It was the subsequent, 1952, examination of relevant discoveries by mathematician Georg Cantor and Bernhard Riemann, which showed this writer the approach which must be adopted for the measurement of this effect.

We summarize here as much of those discoveries as are indispensable for defining that machine-tool principle upon which all successfully sustained (e.g., profitable) performance of agro-industrial economies depends.

The approach to measurement of economic progress depends upon the mastery of Plato's conception of hypothesis, especially as this conception applies to the distinction between Euclidean and non-Euclidean geometries. Riemann was the first to solve the crucial epistemological and formal issues of such distinctions.

Summarily, the application of the Socratic dialectical method to any mutually not-inconsistent array of propositions in geometry, leads to adducing an underlying set of definitions, axioms, and postulates. All possible propositions which are not inconsistent with each and all of the set of definitions, axioms, and postulates, constitutes a *theorem-lattice*; the set of definitions, axioms, and postulates, so employed, constitutes an *hypothesis*. There is no system of mathematical, or other thought, which is not determined, so, by an efficiently determining, underlying hypothesis.

In economics, as in experimental physics generally, any fact of nature which can not be made efficiently consistent with existing generally accepted physical assumptions, constitutes a paradox: the fact exists, in stubborn defiance of pre-existing opinion's most hysterical efforts to deny the very possibility of its existence. Such paradoxes are the stuff of which valid experimental physics, and economics, is made.

In the history of experimental physics, each such paradox has the following general form. According to existing physics doctrine, the fact is an impossibility. Yet, even though the fact ridicules that aspect of existing opinion, existing opinion also contains a lot of efficient truth. Thus, physics (or economics) progresses through two most indispensable steps. The first step, is to define the principle of nature which the paradox expresses. The second step, once an experimentally valid principle has been adduced, is to create a new hypothesis, to supersede the hypothesis underlying the old scientific knowledge. We can not simply add the new principle to the old hypothesis, we must generate an entirely new hypothesis, in consideration of the way in which the newly discovered principle impacts each and every item of definition, axiom, and postulate of the superseded hypothesis.

Since Riemann's 1854 habilitation dissertation,[15] the difference between two successive such hypotheses of experimental physics is considered as a change in the "curvature" of physical space-time. For example, one might say, that any individual act taken upon a flat Earth's surface, would have a different characteristic result than the same apparent action taken on the surface of the ellipsoid Earth; we would also say, with Kepler, Carl Gauss, and Riemann, that the preference for elliptic, rather than circular solar orbits, references a relative difference in every action taken within the solar system. Such, roughly, are the implications of the same form of work performed by an individual in a national economy characterized by one set of technologies, and the same

---

15. Bernhard Riemann, *"Über die Hypothesen, welche der Geometrie zu Grunde liegen"*, **Bernhard Riemanns Gesammelte Mathematische Werke**, H. Weber, ed., second edition (New York: Dover Publications, 1953).

form of work, by the same individual, in a national economy characterized by a different set of technologies. The fact that the individual action's significance varies according to the context in which it occurs, is a notion belonging to the domain of *Analysis Situs*.

The economic requirement that every young person in modern society must enjoy a Classical humanist form of education, rather than that "textbook" education generally employed in schools today, is that knowledge of a valid principle of nature can be imparted to a person *in no other way* than the method central to such a humanist education. The student must be confronted by a paradox, which confounds what the student has believed up to that moment. The student must overcome that paradox by generating the solution to the paradox, not through receipt of "information," but only through reenacting a relevant original discoverer's original act of discovery within the sovereign cognitive processes of the student's own, utterly private mental processes. What a student has learned in that way, the student actually knows; what he has learned to identify by textbook methods of education, he does not actually know. In the latter case, he, or she is merely gossiping about what they read, or heard some place.

If a student comes to know a succession of many valid conceptions of discovered principles in a Classical-humanist way, the student also knows something much more fundamental than any of those learned principles. The student whose education has been centered on privately reenacting a succession of valid solutions to crucial paradoxes—as if thus, to reexperience much of the history of human knowledge, has come to master the use of that principle of his, or her own private mental life, a principle whose common quality is that it is the efficient means by which a succession of valid original discoveries of principle was reenacted. This principle is identified by Plato as *higher hypothesis*. In Riemannian physics, this *higher hypothesis* corresponds to the ordering-principle underlying a succession of valid discoveries of principle, an ordering-principle in the changing curvature of physical space-time, for example. This training of the student, is the production of the adult person capable of assimilating and generating valid principled solutions to problems with which that student has never been confronted before.[16]

How the Machine-Tool Principle Is Situated

---

16. For example, in a competently run classroom, no written or oral examination fails to feature demanded answers for questions in which the student has had no preparation during the relevant preceding classes,

Philip Ulanowsky

A summer-camp science class with nuclear scientist Dr. Robert Moon, who helped the students re-create some of the fundamental electrodynamic experiments of nineteenth-century French scientist André-Marie Ampère, including the making of the experimental equipment.

changes in an efficient way.

It is those directions of change in the technological environment of education and production, which increase the net productive powers of labor, per capita, per household, and per square kilometer. Without those changes, reversing the entropy of technological attrition, the economic process would be as characteristically an "entropic zero-sum game" as the quackery of systems analysis presumes. It is those creative powers of the individual human mind, the same which define man as in the image of the Creator, which are the sole source of sustainable profit (e.g., sustainable not-entropy) in economies.

Thus, the rate of improvement in the characteristic conditions of life-in-general of entire societies, is in proportion to the extent and quality of compulsory universal education, and to the fostering of scientific and technological progress (and, also, related Classical forms of artistic progress) in development of the preconditions for increases of the productive powers of labor. Those preconditions feature basic economic infrastructure (itself chiefly the responsibility of government), the fostering of investment in capital-intensive, power-intensive modes of scientific and technological progress, and the ratio of the number of persons employed in the strategic sector of the machine-tool industry, relative to the total number of well-educated operatives employed in agriculture and industry.

Classical humanist education in reexperiencing many of the most important valid, original discoveries of past history, up to the present; it is the key to competence in comprehending history itself; and, it is the prerequisite for the aptitudes qualifying the matured student for employment in an environment of technologically progressive production. This is also the method for developing those moral qualities of the individual person which reflect the fact that he, or she is made in the image of the Creator. Any other form of education, or very little education, is a cruel, very un-American cheating of the individual by the society.

This quality of education is the companion of Classical forms of scientific and artistic progress (as opposed to the grunt, sweat, screech, and howl alternatives). Such education is associated with scientific progress; from such a symbiosis of education and science, society obtains the principles which revolutionize the strategic machine-tool sector, and the labor-force which is qualified to assimilate those revolutionary

Those latter, summary considerations show us why the economy associated with the A.D. 1471-1966 development of the modern European form of nation-state, had, despite all contrary, negative features of European civilization, improved the demographic conditions of life of the world's population more than all forms of culture before it, each and all taken together. The core of this superiority of that form of national economy is located predominantly within the principles of: 1) universally compulsory Classical humanist education; 2) fostering of investment in capital-intensive, power-intensive modes of increase in the productive powers of labor; 3) fostering of high rates of transmission of valid new discoveries of principle into the productive process and product designs at the relatively highest rate, as through a high-density role of the

---

or within the textbooks and other references assigned during those classes. The question is not how much the student retains from education degraded into a mere rehearsal for filling-out mutiple-choice questionnaires; the question is, how well has the student's mind been developed for solving specific classes of problems which the student has not confronted earlier? That is the difference between the student who knows, and the parrot-like drudge, who has virtually memorized the algorithms in textbook and class notes.

strategic machine-tool design-sector in respect to per-capita productive output.

What Went Awry

Since the 1471-1966 development of nation-state economy, such as the United States and Germany, and Meiji Restoration Japan, Sun Yat-sen's community of followers on Taiwan, and so on, has performed so well, why should any sane person have wished to impede the spread and acceleration of these benefits to all mankind? Briefly, the modern nation-state, as it emerged in western Europe during the Fifteenth Century, occurred within a world at large which was dominated by an incumbent set of ruling oligarchies, both landed aristocracies and financier nobilities such as those of ancient Tyre and medieval Venice. The subsequent five and a half centuries, since the Great Council of Florence, have been a bloody war, fought upon a planet-wide stage, between two irreconcilably opposing principles: the society belonging to the citizen, versus a rule over mankind by the entrenched, landed, and especially, the financier oligarchies.

During the Seventeenth and Eighteenth Centuries, the emerging center of oligarchical power was shifted from Venice and the Habsburgs, to the maritime financier oligarchies of William of Orange's Netherlands and London. This latter, oligarchical faction was known throughout Europe of those centuries, as "the Venetian Party."

Exemplary of the war which the Venetian Party fought in the attempt to destroy the work of Leibniz, is the Europe-wide network of salons, known as the Enlightenment, established under the direction of Venice's Paris-based spy-master Antonio Conti. Voltaire is exemplary of Conti's assets. One of the key centers of the Conti network's efforts to eradicate the influence of its leading adversary of the time, Gottfried Leibniz, was an institution established by Leibniz himself, the Academy of Science in Frederick the Great's Berlin. From the arrival of the Swiss mathematician and fanatical Newton-cultist, Leonhard Euler, at this Academy, in 1741, through the death of Frederick and the 1787 departure of Euler's successor, Joseph Lagrange, this Academy was the center of production of a series of gigantic hoaxes, mostly directed against Leibniz and Leibniz's co-thinkers. Through a hoax perpetrated against Leibniz's ***Monadology***, and against science, by Euler himself, Euler's ***Letters to a German Princess***, all modern science was set back since, through a doctrine enshrined in Lagrange's dogma respecting analytical functions, the fraudulent presumption that physics is mathematically linear in the very small.

The influence of Euler on the doctrine of his contemporary, Immanuel Kant, was enormous. The entirety of the famous four *Critiques* of Immanuel Kant, is derived from the tautological fraud at the center of Euler's ***Letters to a German Princess***. Thus, it was the writer's adolescent battling against Kant which provided the training for attacking the neo-Kantian frauds at the center of the hoaxes of Norbert Wiener and John von Neumann.

The essential, common fraud of Euler, Lagrange, Kant, Bertrand Russell, and Russell's students Wiener and von Neumann, is the assumption, that any valid discovery in physical science might be derived from the kind of mathematical formalism consistent with the assumptions of Eulerian infinite series: linearization in the very small. In this kind of mathematics, the real world of Carl F. Gauss and Bernhard Riemann is presumed to be non-existent. No principle of hypothesis is allowed. In short, the kind of mathematics associated with the Conti-Euler-Kant tradition substitutes for the real universe, a fictitious, mathematical universe, a mere *virtual reality*. For these empiricists, as for Thomas Hobbes before them, metaphor is not permitted; valid cognitive discoveries of principles of nature, are denied, as Kant denies them.

The included outcome is the absurdity which passes for economic theory in the classroom and boardroom today, a virtual-reality economic process, in which the role of the cognitive powers of the individual person is allowed no efficient functional expression in the account given.

The centuries-long issue is simply this. To have a progressing form of modern nation-state economy, it is indispensable to provide compulsory and universal, Classical humanist forms of education, and to provide the vocations and circumstances in society suited to the needs of those young and matured persons who are products of such education. In such a society a parasitical oligarchy of the "Venetian Party" type ruling London and Wall Street today, would not be tolerated. The leading oligarchical intelligentsia are not so ignorant as to believe, themselves, what they would have our Congress, and you, to believe. They know that our form of economy has worked brilliantly, and would do so again; they know that their neo-Malthusian model is an economic catastrophe; but, they also know, that under a successful society, the power of parasitical oligarchies to rule the nation and and world would soon come to an end. They would prefer "to reign in Hell, than be a mere citizen in Heaven."

Rebuild Puerto Rico and All North America with 'New Silk Road' Paradigm

by Marcia Merry Baker and Paul Gallagher

Oct. 1—Puerto Rico is in the forefront of world attention, because of the near-total destruction of its baseline infrastructure by Hurricanes Irma and Maria, affecting 3.4 million people, which demands credit creation and follow-through for building a whole new economy on the island.

The same is required for locations suffering destruction in September, all across the mid-latitudes of the American Hemisphere, stretching from earthquakes in Pacific Mexico, to the hurricane belt reaching to the Caribbean's Leeward Islands, with the U.S. Gulf States in between. The combined population affected by disasters is in the range of 90 millions of people, hit either directly or close-by, in multiple U.S. states and territories, Mexican states, and the islands.

The time period of the disasters: Hurricane Harvey (Aug. 17-Sept. 3), Hurricane Irma (Aug. 30-Sept. 16), Hurricane José (Sept. 5-26), Hurricane Maria (Sept. 16 to Oct. 1); the Pacific Rim of Fire quakes were in September—off the Oaxaca coast, in Mexico City and elsewhere. The scale of the death, dislocation, and destruction is so great that no boot-strap approach to recovery can work.

The obvious challenge in building up Puerto Rico, in restoring Texas and Florida to a higher level, and dealing with the other disasters, is to scale up *the entire U.S. economy.* Moreover, it is urgent to thoroughly modernize New York City's aged infrastructure, especially transportation, which was made even worse by Hurricane Sandy in 2012, and has not been up-graded. For such epic rebuilding, the volume of steel, heavy machinery, transportation infrastructure, and other essential inputs needed, requires rebuilding the entire *non-disaster zone* of the rest of the U.S. economy, which is a wreck from neglect.

How to do this, is the role of a *LaRouche Plan of Action* response to the disasters; the plan was issued Aug. 31, after the first landfall by Hurricane Harvey in Texas. In brief, it calls for putting into place the Four Laws, first issued by LaRouche in June 2014, to restore the U.S. economy: (1) reinstate Glass-Steagall to restore sound banking; (2) set up a national bank for large-scale credit; (3) issue credit and launch priority projects; and (4) back science driver programs, especially in space and fusion energy.

Most important is to link up with the "New Silk Road" of infrastructure building initiated in Eurasia, as of Fall, 2013, when China's President Xi Jinping called for a New Silk Road "Belt" of overland development

Hurricane Maria devastated homes and infrastructure in Puerto Rico.

Puerto Rico's electricity infrastructure has been destroyed.

corridors, and a "Maritime Silk Road." The principles involved are economic development and peace. The Chinese, with Russia, are acting on these principles in what's called the "BRI"—Belt and Road Initiative, whose first world forum was last May in Beijing.

Look, for example, at what is now happening in Haiti—right in the center of America's hurricane and earthquake zone. China and the Mayor of Port au Prince have announced a multi-billion dollar program to rebuild the city and hinterlands, including storm defenses, power and water supplies, safe residences all to a new, productive level. Ccontrast that with the Obama Administration's flat refusal to take an "Army Corps of Engineers" approach to save and rebuild in Haiti after the 2010 earthquake, which has resulted in disease and suffering over the last seven years.

Individual U.S. states arc now lining up to make their own economic arrangements with China. Illinois Governor Bruce Rauner said in Chicago Sept. 28, "I'm a believer in more trade and more investment, especially with the people of China." He led a delegation there in September. Illinois' agro-industrial decline and infrastructure decay are so bad, the state is suffering absolute population loss. Other recent U.S. delegations to China include officials from Montana, Michigan and Iowa.

To rebuild in Puerto Rico, Texas, Florida, Mexico, the Caribbean and throughout the whole disaster zone, bring the Silk Road to the Americas! Within six weeks, President Trump will be in China to meet President Xi Jinping. Let this be the beginning of a new era.

Infrastructure Discussion

The reason three major American metropolitan areas were devastated in little over a decade—New Orleans (2005), New York City (2012), and Houston (2017), and now the entire island of Puerto Rico—is the lack of protective infrastructure *engineered decades earlier*, but never built, due to Wall Street's increasing control over U.S. economic policy for the past half century. Finally, the first beginnings of a paradigm shift have been provoked.

In the White House, sources say that an intense discussion is taking place of the "trillion-dollar infrastructure-building program" now stalled for nine long months on the Trump agenda. President Trump himself wrote Sept. 29 on Twitter, "The fact is that Puerto Rico has been destroyed by two hurricanes. Big decisions will have to be made as to the cost of its rebuilding."

The President "swung strongly away last week from the model of public-private partnerships to build projects," one source said, speaking of a Sept. 26 bi-partisan White House meeting. A Democratic Congressman reported that President Trump committed in that meeting to public funding of the entire infrastructure-building program, although he was undecided on *how* this would be funded. The same week, Rep. Peter DeFazio, Ranking Member on the House Transportation and Infrastructure Committee, told reporters Sept. 28, that he spoke to President Trump's infrastructure adviser, D.J. Gribbin, stressing that House Democrats are willing to work with the White House, and even the Freedom Caucus, on infrastructure. He said, if they want infrastructure investment, "We have bills that they would support, that we would support."

Thus, "action, and action now" on new infrastructure projects, for both protection and productivity, has entered the minds of elected officials, as *EIR* representatives found even in offices of Congress during this same week. Mentioning the very subject enabled unscheduled and sometimes lengthy meetings with senior Congressional staff and/or members. As intense as the focus often appeared, any idea of how to finance this new infrastructure and technology was utterly lacking.

Link with Belt and Road

Here is where the link-up with the China-launched Belt and Road Initiative—which is building major new infrastructure projects across four continents—was proposed as critical by *EIR* representatives. This link is the clear solution, but means that a United States national credit institution, lacking for 60 years, is as vital as a national capital budget, not used for 45.

A useful op-ed in the Sept. 17 *Houston Chronicle* asked, "What would Jesse Jones do?" really posing the question, that if the United States now had a large-scale national lending institution like President Franklin Roosevelt's Reconstruction Finance Corporation (RFC) which Jones headed, what could it do, to reverse the devastation on the Texas Gulf Coast and prevent it's happening again? In Roosevelt's Presidency, disasters such as these were not called "natural," but the result of "human greed and neglect," i.e., Wall Street policy, which had prevented the building of defensive infrastructure then, and continues to prevent it today because it "costs too much."

The *LaRouche Plan of Action* proposes specifically a Hamiltonian national bank for infrastructure and manufacturing, by which $1-2 trillion in outstanding Treasury debt would be exchanged for longer-term equity in the Bank, and similarly large volumes of credit issued as currency by the Bank, for the productive, and pressing, high-technology new infrastructure. Such Treasury debt for national bank equity could immediately involve large foreign Treasury bondholders as well—China and Japan—as can easily be confirmed. This helps open the American door to the New Silk Road, and to great projects both here, and bridging to Mexico/South America and to Canada/Alaska/Eurasia, and finally, to joint reconstruction of Mideast and North African nations destroyed by Bush's and Obama's wars.

This idea—combined with Glass-Steagall reinstatement to restore sound banking, and space and fusion science "drivers," has been presented time and again in many Congressional offices, but seemed, this week, to be "heard" for the first time, and as something new and surprising. This reflects the combined impact of the epic disasters, and the national solidarity impulse of the

American population to instinctively volunteer help, and to instinctively want real rebuilding, not fake "recovery."

What it will take is the American System of economy, more than two centuries old, and developed now to a higher level through implementing LaRouche's Four Laws to save the nation. It will take more popular mobilization before the incipient debate among decision-makers becomes meaningful, but it is the only course of action, and can be done.

Puerto Rico, First Response

Puerto Rico stands out, not only because of the horrible Hurricane Maria destruction, but for the fact that its economy was already in decline and turmoil when, in Spring 2016, the situation was deliberately worsened by the Obama Administration's demand for debt-austerity, under the PROMESA plan. This was forced through Congress to satisfy Wall Street. Every infrastructure sector was already outmoded and in decay, from the Puerto Rico Electric Power Authority (PREPA) to the 38 dams on the rivers, all classified as "high hazard potential," for want of strengthening and replacement. There existed no railroad at all, only the 10.7 mile Tren Urbano light transit system serving San Juan, Guaynabo and Bayamon. While the Port of San Juan handled a significant volume of cargo, no significant processing centers had been built up in association with this. Puerto Ricans have been leaving their homeland. The population fell by 334,000 in the 15 years from 2000 to 2015, down to 3.47 million.

Following Hurricane Irma, Puerto Rico was decimated by Hurricane Maria. All electricity went down. The roadways became impassable from debris and collapsed bridges. Homes, other buildings, and government services structures were destroyed in massive numbers by flooding and winds. Water supplies were knocked out. The 69 hospitals were hit. In effect, battleground conditions were created. The same for the U.S. Virgin Islands and other islands struck by Irma and/or Maria.

Rightly, the response has been military. In the early days, a command structure was put into effect, to conduct the first-phase functions of rescue and emergency relief. Even before this, prior to Maria, FEMA already had its largest pre-storm deployment on the ground on Puerto Rico—a contingent of 300 staff and another 200 search and rescue, plus 100 partnering staff from the Defense Department.

The U.S. Army Corps of Engineers (USACE) is in

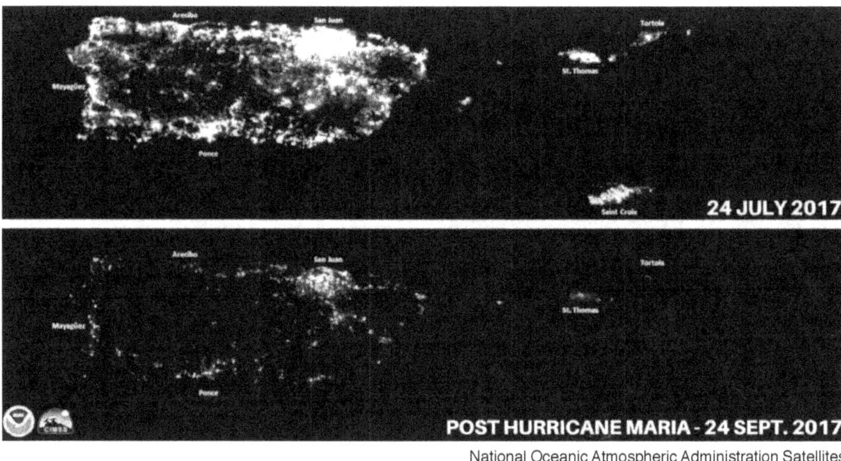

National Oceanic Atmospheric Administration Satellites

Satellite night images of Puerto Rico before and after Hurricane Maria knocked out the power grid, leaving millions without electricity.

charge of power restoration, and is also assigned to shore up the Guajataca Dam, the island's largest dam, which is threatening to break because of the flooding. (A spillway has broken.) FEMA and Homeland Security, along with those—very few—able to participate from the 78 Puerto Rican municipalities, are seeing to water, food and commodity distribution, and the restoration of what can be made viable in the hospital system. The various branches of the military, including the Coast Guard and National Guard, are supporting all these functions, with special responsibility for restoring highways, ports, airports and communications. Their mission also includes sequencing supplies and logistics, so that larger contingents of military and civilian help can be accommodated. The deployments of military ships, helicopters, planes, portable water and power systems, and assets of all kinds is unprecedented.

Build a New Puerto Rico

Next will come the stabilization phase, in which vital functions and services all across the island are expected to be in place, to operate on a continuing basis. This is a gargantuan task. As of the end of September, the military command reported that initial debris-clearing of perimeter roadways was nearly completed, with more work to be done to restore roads in the interior, and in difficult mountainous areas. FEMA will pay 100%

of these costs (unlike a percentage payment in Texas or Florida).

Eleven large commodity distribution sites are in operation—to supply local distribution depots, with a goal of having 25 to 30 up and running by the week of Oct. 2, and also to have the logistics set up for large-scale delivery and stockage. On medical care, work continues to bring up as much of the functioning of the 69 hospitals as possible. As well, the *USNS Comfort* hospital ship, with 1,000 beds and full services, will be on hand in early October. Transportation grants so far include $42 million (Federal Highway Authority) for roads; and $8.4 million for Tren Urbano, as well as for bringing in trucks, drivers and fuel. So far, over 90% of the population still has no electricity; and under 50% have safe water. For some time, "stabilization" will mean only a patchwork of diesel generators, very limited central power service, and makeshift water supplies, including bottled water.

Then what? It is clear that the building phase for Puerto Rico cannot be either an extrapolation of the prior emergency relief and stabilization periods, nor can it be left to the "markets" to decide what gets built or not, as is insanely assumed to be the case for Texas and Florida right now.

Here again the "Belt and Road Initiative" is the

Xinhua/Yang Shiyao

To move non-capital functions out of Beijing, the government of China announced plans April 1 for construction of Xiongan New Area, a new metropolis that will span Xiongxian, Rongcheng (above) and Anxin counties in Hebei Province southwest of Beijing.

SMRs are attracting the attention of government officials, regulators, and energy leaders as a potential addition to the nation's energy mix. Because of their small size - less than 300 MWe, compared to a typical nuclear power plant of 1,000 MWe

At 50 MWe (gross), the NuScale Power Module™ is the smallest of the light water SMRs.

Nuscale Power

The Small Modular Reactor shown here could generate electricity in locations where there is no power, or areas where power has been disrupted.

touchstone. The new cities and economic zones being built along the Eurasian Corridors provide examples of planning and building "from the ground up," for modern, productive, and beautiful spaces.

Several features are special for Puerto Rico. Railroads must be built, for the first time ever, to create an island-wide network, connecting to the ports, and to local roadway systems. For plentiful power, including for electified rail, nuclear reactors are essential. On Sept. 26, Energy Secretary Rick Perry spoke of this, advocating SMRs—small modular nuclear reactors.

One unique opportunity is to build up Ponce—what was Puerto Rico's second largest city, which already has seen itself as the "Port of the Americas." It has deep-water access, and is strategically located near the Mona Passage—the strait where the Atlantic Ocean comes into the Caribbean. This puts Puerto Rico on the map of the world Maritime Silk Road.

Texas, Florida, New York City

The same principles in order for Puerto Rico, also hold for rebuilding, and building anew, in Texas, Florida and the other hurricane disaster zones, espe-

cially for greater New York City. New York/New Jersey was never rehabilitated after Hurricane Sandy in 2012. This storm, on top of the pre-existing decay in the aged transportation system of the region, has resulted in today's catastrophe-waiting-to-happen. A small first step in facing this came in the recent approval of $900 million in Federal funds for the Gateway Project, to build two new rail tunnels under the Hudson River, and a new mainline rail bridge in New Jersey.

To begin with, build the storm-defense infrastructure. In New York/New Jersey, proposals for sea surge barrier systems were once again reviewed in May of this year, at a conference sponsored by the Port Authority of New York and New Jersey. These defenses are long overdue. In 2009, the American Society of Civil Engineers hosted experts proposing protective sea walls for New York, which, had they been built, would have prevented a huge amount of the damage from Sandy three years later.

In southeast Texas, there are key locations along the Gulf Coast for which sea surge barriers are appropriate, and proposals exist, along with flood-water control sys-

U.S. Army Corps of Engineers

Aerial view of the port at Ponce, on the southern shore of Puerto Rico.

tems. Sea surge barriers are also in order for certain places in Florida, such as Jacksonville.

The one shining example of such a piece of infrastructure is the Lake Borgne barrier, near New Orleans, finished in 2011 under authority of the Army Corps of Engineers, after the 2005 Hurricane Katrina disaster.

Florida otherwise, as a low-lying peninsula, presents special challenges for defense against flooding. However, systems of diversion and impoundment can be implemented to lessen damage, as well as to protect life.

Citrus grove damage caused by Hurricane Irma in Immokalee, Florida.

Apart from storm vulnerability, one challenge common to coastal Texas and Florida, is to secure water supplies. With dry spells frequent in Texas, nuclear-powered desalination on the coast would end the problem. As Governor of Texas (2000-2015), Rick Perry, now national Energy Secretary, raised this proposal. In Florida, obtaining good water is a worsening problem, after centuries of well drawdowns have led to widespread salt-water intrusion on the peninsula's coast. Again, with nuclear-powered desalination, the problem is solved.

The prospect of rebuilding these states and other disaster areas on this higher level of infrastructure—along with Puerto Rico, the Caribbean and the Mexican earthquake zones—directly calls the question for dumping the anti-development premises and policies of the last half century, as embodied, for example, in the North American Free Trade Agreement (NAFTA), begun in 1994. The Wall Street and the City of London financial centers forced the enactment of NAFTA, in order to force the relocation of economic activity—manufacturing, textiles, farming, food processing—to whatever new, low-cost production sites would provide the most profiteering for Wall Street. So, U.S. assembly plants, agriculture, and much more left the U.S. for Mexico; and meanwhile, Mexico was forced to become dependent on the U.S. Farmbelt for daily food—corn, beans, wheat. This was to the detriment of all populations involved.

Now we must seize the opportunity afforded by the need to rebuild after these disasters, to return to national sovereignty—with Mexico, the United States, and Canada all working together to build up their economies for the good of all North America, in the Silk Road spirit. The next Canada-Mexico-U.S. NAFTA talks are set for Oct. 11-15 in Washington. The Trump-initiated review of NAFTA, currently in progress, is the occasion to go all the way and end the economic degradation of North America.

The emergency case of agriculture in Florida illustrates the point. Florida has traditionally been a national asset for fresh fruits and vegetables. But under NAFTA, a significant number of Florida producers were put out of business, as production was relocated to Mexico, because of "cheaper" labor, land, water and processing costs. Of no benefit to the Mexican people, the for-export produce (onions, broccoli, tomatoes, berries, etc.) uses scarce water, and is otherwise part of the scheme to make Mexico dependent on "cheaper" U.S. corn and other staples, once grown abundantly in Mexico. The same has happened in Texas and elsewhere, and there are parallels in manufacturing.

Florida citrus growers, whose acreage has already declined significantly over the NAFTA years, now face huge losses of their crops, from 30-100% from region to region, and widespread destruction of trees from winds and standing water. The damage is "somewhere between significant and catastrophic," said the Executive Director of the Florida Department of Citrus, Shannon Shepp, of the storm's impact. Florida tomato growers, and other producers, likewise face huge crop losses, and damage to fields, after years of declining acreage.